LEARNING SQL
Master SQL Fundamentals

Kiet Huynh

Table of Contents

PART I
Introduction to SQL

1.1 SQL and Databases

SQL (Structured Query Language) is a powerful tool for managing and manipulating data in relational database management systems (RDBMS). In this section, we will provide an overview of SQL and its relationship with databases.

What is SQL?

SQL is a domain-specific language used for interacting with databases. It allows users to perform a wide range of operations on data, including retrieving, inserting, updating, and deleting records. SQL provides a standardized way to communicate with databases, making it possible to work with various database systems like MySQL, PostgreSQL, Oracle, and Microsoft SQL Server.

Databases and Data Management

Databases are organized collections of data that are structured in a way that allows for efficient storage, retrieval, and management of information. They serve as the backbone of many applications and systems, storing everything from user profiles on a social media platform to financial records in an enterprise environment.

The Relational Model

One of the most common database models is the relational model, where data is organized into tables or relations. Each table consists of rows (records) and columns (attributes). SQL is particularly well-suited for working with relational databases.

Why Learn SQL?

Learning SQL is essential for anyone who deals with data. Whether you are a data analyst, a software developer, or a business intelligence professional, SQL is a fundamental skill. Here are some reasons why learning SQL is important:

1. Data Retrieval: SQL allows you to extract specific information from a database quickly and efficiently. For example, you can retrieve a list of customers who made a purchase in the last month.

2. Data Modification: You can insert, update, and delete data in a database using SQL. This is crucial for maintaining the accuracy and integrity of your data.

3. Data Analysis: SQL provides powerful tools for data analysis, including aggregating data, performing calculations, and generating reports.

4. Database Administration: If you work in IT, knowing SQL is essential for tasks such as database setup, maintenance, and optimization.

5. Integration: SQL can be integrated into various programming languages, allowing developers to build applications that interact with databases seamlessly.

Getting Started with SQL

To begin your journey with SQL, you'll need access to a database system. Many RDBMS options are available, and you can choose one that suits your needs. For learning purposes, you can start with SQLite, which is a self-contained, serverless, and zero-configuration database engine.

Here are the steps to get started:

1. Install an RDBMS: Download and install an RDBMS software such as MySQL, PostgreSQL, or SQLite, depending on your preference.

2. Install a SQL Client: You'll need a tool to write and execute SQL queries. Popular SQL clients include MySQL Workbench, DBeaver, and SQLite Studio.

3. Create a Database: Using your SQL client, create a new database. You can think of a database as a container for your data.

4. Create Tables: Inside your database, create tables to structure your data. Define the columns (fields) and their data types.

5. Insert Data: Populate your tables with data using SQL INSERT statements. You can start with simple data, such as a list of employees or products.

6. Query Data: Write SQL SELECT queries to retrieve information from your tables. For example, you can retrieve a list of all employees or find products with a specific price range.

As you progress, you'll learn more SQL commands, including those for updating and deleting data. Additionally, you'll explore advanced SQL topics like joins, aggregations, and subqueries, which are crucial for querying and analyzing complex datasets.

Remember that practice is key to mastering SQL. The more you work with databases and write SQL queries, the more proficient you'll become. In the following sections of this book, we will delve deeper into SQL concepts and provide hands-on examples to help you build your SQL skills.

1.2. History and Evolution of SQL

To truly understand SQL (Structured Query Language) and its significance in modern database management, it's essential to explore its rich history and evolution. SQL has come a long way since its inception, shaping the database industry and becoming a cornerstone of data management.

The Birth of SQL: The 1970s

SQL's history dates back to the early 1970s when IBM researchers Raymond Boyce and Donald Chamberlin began working on a project called "System R" at IBM's San Jose Research Laboratory. Their goal was to develop a standardized method for interacting with relational databases.

In 1974, Boyce and Chamberlin published a groundbreaking paper titled "A Relational Model of Data for Large Shared Data Banks," which introduced the relational model—a fundamental concept underlying SQL. The paper laid the foundation for the concepts of tables, rows, and columns as a way to organize data.

Structured English Query Language (SEQUEL): The Early Days

The original name for SQL was "Structured English Query Language" (SEQUEL). However, due to trademark issues, it was later renamed "SQL." In the mid-1970s, IBM began implementing the SEQUEL language on its System R project.

SQL Becomes an Industry Standard: The 1980s

SQL's popularity grew rapidly, and in the 1980s, it became an industry standard. This development was largely due to the efforts of the American National Standards Institute (ANSI) and the International Organization for Standardization (ISO), which worked together to define a standardized SQL specification.

The first official SQL standard was published by ANSI in 1986. This standardization ensured that SQL could be used across various database systems, promoting interoperability and ease of use.

SQL in the Real World: Commercial Database Systems

As SQL gained prominence, commercial database management systems (DBMS) incorporating SQL emerged. Some of the early DBMS that utilized SQL included IBM's DB2, Oracle, and Microsoft's SQL Server. These systems provided robust platforms for managing large datasets and allowed organizations to leverage SQL for data manipulation.

SQL-89 and SQL-92 Standards

In 1989, ANSI released the SQL-89 standard, followed by the SQL-92 standard in—you guessed it—1992. These standards continued to refine SQL's capabilities and introduced new features like outer joins and support for referential integrity constraints. SQL-92 remains a significant milestone in SQL's history and forms the basis for many modern database systems.

The Rise of Open-Source Database Systems

The late 1990s and early 2000s witnessed the rise of open-source database systems that supported SQL. MySQL, PostgreSQL, and SQLite became popular choices for developers and organizations seeking cost-effective and scalable database solutions. These open-source systems contributed to SQL's widespread adoption.

In recent years, SQL has adapted to meet the challenges posed by big data and NoSQL databases. New SQL standards, such as SQL:2003, SQL:2008, and SQL:2011, introduced features for working with XML data, enhanced window functions, and improved support for recursive queries.

Additionally, SQL-based querying languages like HiveQL and Spark SQL have emerged to handle large-scale data processing in the context of big data technologies like Apache Hadoop and Apache Spark.

Conclusion

SQL has come a long way since its inception in the 1970s. From its humble beginnings as SEQUEL to becoming a globally recognized standard, SQL has revolutionized the way we manage and interact with data. Its evolution continues as it adapts to the demands of modern data processing and analytics.

As you delve deeper into SQL in this book, you'll explore its various aspects and learn how to harness its power for data manipulation and analysis. Understanding SQL's history provides valuable context for appreciating its significance in today's data-driven world.

1.3. Common Database Management Systems

In the world of database management, several Database Management Systems (DBMS) play a prominent role. These systems are the backbone of data storage, retrieval, and manipulation, and they provide the foundation upon which SQL operates. In this section, we will explore some of the most common DBMS platforms and their significance in the SQL landscape.

1. Relational Database Management Systems (RDBMS)

Relational Database Management Systems, or RDBMS, are the most prevalent type of DBMS. They use a structured approach to data storage, where information is organized into tables with rows and columns. Here are a few of the most widely used RDBMS platforms:

1.1. MySQL:

- MySQL is an open-source RDBMS known for its speed, reliability, and ease of use.

- It is commonly used in web applications and is the database system behind popular content management systems like WordPress.

- MySQL supports SQL for data manipulation and offers robust security features.

1.2. PostgreSQL:

- PostgreSQL is a powerful open-source RDBMS known for its extensibility and support for complex data types.

- It is often chosen for applications requiring advanced features and custom extensions.

- PostgreSQL is fully ACID compliant (Atomicity, Consistency, Isolation, Durability) and offers a wide range of SQL capabilities.

1.3. Oracle Database:

- Oracle Database is a commercial RDBMS widely used in enterprise environments.

- It offers features like high availability, scalability, and advanced security options.

- Oracle Database supports SQL and has its own variations of SQL called PL/SQL for procedural programming.

1.4. Microsoft SQL Server:

- Microsoft SQL Server is a popular RDBMS used primarily in Windows environments.

- It integrates seamlessly with other Microsoft products and offers strong support for business intelligence and reporting.

- SQL Server provides a comprehensive set of tools for database management and development.

2. NoSQL Database Management Systems

While RDBMS systems dominate the database landscape, NoSQL (Not Only SQL) databases have gained prominence, especially in scenarios where flexibility and scalability are crucial. Here are a couple of notable NoSQL categories:

2.1. Document Databases:

- Document databases store data in semi-structured documents, often using formats like JSON or BSON.

- MongoDB is a popular document database known for its flexibility and ease of scalability.

- SQL-like querying is possible in some document databases, making them relevant to SQL users.

2.2. Key-Value Stores:

- Key-value stores are designed for high-speed retrieval of simple data structures.

- Redis is a widely used key-value store known for its blazing-fast performance and support for various data structures.

- While they lack SQL querying capabilities, key-value stores are valuable in specific use cases like caching.

3. NewSQL Databases

NewSQL databases aim to combine the best of both worlds—combining the scalability of NoSQL with the reliability and querying capabilities of SQL. Some examples include Google Spanner and CockroachDB.

4. In-Memory Databases

In-memory databases store data in the server's main memory (RAM) rather than on disk, offering extremely fast data access. Examples include Redis (also mentioned earlier) and Apache Ignite.

5. Columnar Databases

Columnar databases store data in columns rather than rows, optimizing for data warehousing and analytical queries. Amazon Redshift and Google BigQuery are popular choices in this category.

Choosing the Right DBMS for Your Needs

Selecting the appropriate DBMS for your project is crucial. Consider the following factors:

1. Data Model: Does your data have a well-defined structure (RDBMS) or is it semi-structured or unstructured (NoSQL)?

2. Scalability: How much data do you need to store, and will your data grow significantly over time?

3. Performance: What are your performance requirements, especially regarding read and write operations?

4. Consistency: Is strong data consistency (ACID compliance) critical for your application?

5. Complex Queries: Will you need complex SQL queries and joins, or can you work with simpler data retrieval?

6. Budget: What are your budget constraints? Commercial RDBMS may have licensing costs.

7. Ecosystem: Consider the tools and libraries available for the DBMS, as well as its integration capabilities with your existing infrastructure.

Understanding the strengths and weaknesses of various DBMS options will help you make an informed decision. As you progress in your SQL journey, you may find yourself working with different DBMS platforms, each tailored to specific project requirements.

PART II
SQL Basics

2.1 The SELECT Statement: Querying Data

In the world of SQL, the SELECT statement is your primary tool for retrieving data from a database. It's the gateway to extracting information that is meaningful and valuable to your applications or analyses. In this section, we will dive into the intricacies of the SELECT statement, providing practical examples and step-by-step instructions.

2.1.1 Using SELECT to Retrieve Data

Understanding the SELECT Statement

The `SELECT` statement is SQL's workhorse for querying data. At its core, it allows you to specify what data you want to retrieve from one or more tables in a database. Let's break down its basic structure:

sql

SELECT column1, column2, ...

FROM table_name;

- `SELECT`: This keyword signals the start of a query.

- `column1, column2, ...`: These are the columns you want to retrieve. You can specify one or more columns, or use `*` to select all columns.

- `FROM`: This keyword specifies the table(s) from which you want to retrieve data.

- `table_name`: Replace this with the name of the table from which you want to fetch data.

Basic SELECT Examples

Let's consider a simple example using a hypothetical "Employees" table. This table might look like this:

EmployeeID	FirstName	LastName	Department
1	John	Smith	Sales
2	Jane	Doe	HR
3	Robert	Johnson	IT

Example 1: Retrieving All Columns

sql

SELECT *

FROM Employees;

In this example, we're using `SELECT *` to fetch all columns from the "Employees" table. The result will include all rows and all columns:

EmployeeID	FirstName	LastName	Department
1	John	Smith	Sales
2	Jane	Doe	HR
3	Robert	Johnson	IT

Example 2: Retrieving Specific Columns

sql

```
SELECT FirstName, LastName
FROM Employees;
```

In this case, we're only interested in the "FirstName" and "LastName" columns. The result will include all rows but only these two columns:

FirstName	LastName
John	Smith
Jane	Doe
Robert	Johnson

Filtering Data with WHERE Clause

Often, you'll want to retrieve specific rows that meet certain criteria. That's where the `WHERE` clause comes into play. It allows you to filter the rows you retrieve based on specified conditions. Let's continue with examples:

Example 3: Using WHERE Clause

sql

SELECT EmployeeID, FirstName, LastName

FROM Employees

WHERE Department = 'HR';

Here, we're retrieving the "EmployeeID," "FirstName," and "LastName" columns for employees who work in the HR department. The `WHERE` clause filters the rows based on the condition `Department = 'HR'`. The result is:

EmployeeID	FirstName	LastName
2	Jane	Doe

Example 4: Complex Conditions with WHERE Clause

sql

SELECT EmployeeID, FirstName, LastName

FROM Employees

WHERE Department = 'IT' OR Department = 'Sales';

In this example, we're retrieving employees from either the IT or Sales departments. We use the `OR` operator in the `WHERE` clause to specify multiple conditions. The result includes employees from both departments:

EmployeeID	FirstName	LastName
1	John	Smith
3	Robert	Johnson

Sorting Data with ORDER BY

SQL allows you to control the order in which data is presented using the `ORDER BY` clause. This clause is often paired with the `SELECT` statement to sort the retrieved data based on one or more columns, either in ascending (default) or descending order.

Example 5: Sorting Data

sql

SELECT EmployeeID, FirstName, LastName, Department

FROM Employees

ORDER BY Department ASC, LastName DESC;

In this example, we're retrieving all columns from the "Employees" table but sorting the results first by the "Department" column in ascending order (`ASC`) and then by the "LastName" column in descending order (`DESC`). The result is:

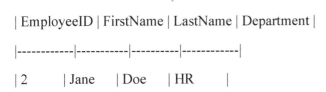

EmployeeID	FirstName	LastName	Department
2	Jane	Doe	HR

| 1 | John | Smith | Sales |
| 3 | Robert | Johnson | IT |

Limiting Results with LIMIT

In situations where you have a large dataset but only want to retrieve a subset of the results, you can use the `LIMIT` clause to restrict the number of rows returned.

Example 6: Limiting Results

sql

```
SELECT EmployeeID, FirstName, LastName
FROM Employees
LIMIT 2;
```

Here, we're retrieving the "EmployeeID,"

 "FirstName," and "LastName" columns but limiting the result to only the first two rows. The output will include the first two employees:

EmployeeID	FirstName	LastName
1	John	Smith
2	Jane	Doe

Conclusion

The `SELECT` statement is the foundation of SQL data retrieval. You've learned how to use it to retrieve specific columns, filter data with the `WHERE` clause, sort results with `ORDER BY`, and limit the number of rows with `LIMIT`. These fundamental SQL skills will serve as the building blocks for more advanced data manipulation and analysis tasks as you continue your SQL journey.

2.1.2 Using DISTINCT to Eliminate Duplicate Rows

In SQL, it's common to encounter situations where your query results include duplicate rows. This can happen when you're working with large datasets or tables that contain redundant information. The **`DISTINCT`** keyword is a powerful tool to remove these duplicates and retrieve only unique records from your query. In this section, we will explore how to use **`DISTINCT`** effectively, along with practical examples and step-by-step instructions.

Understanding Duplicate Rows

Duplicate rows in a query result occur when there are multiple identical records in the table you're querying. These duplicates can skew your analysis and make your data harder to work with. Let's consider a simple example using a "Customers" table:

CustomerID	FirstName	LastName	Email
1	John	Smith	john@example.com
2	Jane	Doe	jane@example.com
3	John	Smith	john@example.com
4	Mary	Johnson	mary@example.com

In this table, we have two duplicate records for John Smith, both with the same email address.

Using DISTINCT

The `DISTINCT` keyword is used in conjunction with the `SELECT` statement to retrieve only unique rows from a query result. It ensures that each row appears in the result set only once, eliminating duplicates.

Basic Usage of DISTINCT

Let's start with a simple example to illustrate the basic usage of `DISTINCT`. We want to retrieve a list of unique email addresses from the "Customers" table:

```sql
SELECT DISTINCT Email
FROM Customers;
```

In this query, we're selecting the "Email" column and applying `DISTINCT` to it. The result will include only unique email addresses:

```
| Email               |
|---------------------|
| john@example.com    |
| jane@example.com    |
```

| mary@example.com |

As you can see, the duplicate email addresses have been eliminated from the result.

Using DISTINCT with Multiple Columns

`DISTINCT` is not limited to a single column; you can apply it to multiple columns to ensure uniqueness across combinations of values. Let's consider an example using both the "FirstName" and "LastName" columns:

sql

```
SELECT DISTINCT FirstName, LastName
FROM Customers;
```

In this query, we're retrieving distinct combinations of first and last names from the "Customers" table. The result will include unique pairs of first and last names:

FirstName	LastName
John	Smith
Jane	Doe
Mary	Johnson

Notice that even though there were duplicate records for John Smith in the original table, the query results contain only one entry for him, as the combination of first and last name is considered.

Using DISTINCT with ORDER BY

You can also combine `DISTINCT` with `ORDER BY` to retrieve unique records while maintaining a specific sorting order. For example, if you want to list all unique cities from the "Customers" table in alphabetical order:

```sql
SELECT DISTINCT City
FROM Customers
ORDER BY City ASC;
```

In this query, we first retrieve the unique cities using `DISTINCT`, and then we apply `ORDER BY` to sort them alphabetically in ascending order. The result will include a list of unique cities:

City
New York
Paris
San Diego

Using DISTINCT with Aggregate Functions

You can leverage `**DISTINCT**` with aggregate functions like `**COUNT**`, `**SUM**`, and `**AVG**` to perform calculations on unique values. For instance, if you want to count the number of unique orders in an "Orders" table:

sql

SELECT COUNT(DISTINCT OrderID)

FROM Orders;

In this example, we use `DISTINCT` with the `COUNT` function to count the number of unique order IDs in the "Orders" table.

Dealing with NULL Values

It's important to note that `DISTINCT` treats NULL values as unique. If you have NULL values in your column, they will be considered distinct from each other and from non-NULL values. For example:

sql

SELECT DISTINCT Department

FROM Employees;

In this query, if the "Department" column contains NULL values, each NULL value will be treated as distinct, resulting in multiple NULL entries in the result.

Conclusion

The `DISTINCT` keyword is a valuable tool in SQL for eliminating duplicate rows from query results. Whether you need to retrieve unique values from a single column or ensure uniqueness across multiple columns, `DISTINCT` allows you to work with cleaner and more meaningful data. As you continue your SQL journey, mastering the use of `DISTINCT` will help you effectively manage and analyze datasets of varying complexity.

2.1.3 Filtering Data with WHERE

In SQL, the `WHERE` clause is a powerful tool that allows you to filter data based on specified conditions. It enables you to retrieve only the rows that meet specific criteria, making your queries more focused and meaningful. In this section, we will explore how to use the `WHERE` clause effectively, providing practical examples and step-by-step instructions.

Understanding the WHERE Clause

The `WHERE` clause is a fundamental component of SQL queries. It allows you to specify conditions that filter the rows returned by your `SELECT` statement. When you apply a `WHERE` clause, only the rows that satisfy the given conditions are included in the query result.

Basic Usage of WHERE

Let's start with a simple example to illustrate the basic usage of the `WHERE` clause. Suppose we have a table called "Employees" with the following data:

EmployeeID	FirstName	LastName	Department	Salary

1	John	Smith	Sales	50000
2	Jane	Doe	HR	45000
3	Robert	Johnson	IT	60000
4	Mary	Johnson	Sales	52000

Example 1: Filtering by a Single Condition

sql

SELECT FirstName, LastName, Department

FROM Employees

WHERE Department = 'Sales';

In this query, we're retrieving the "FirstName," "LastName," and "Department" columns from the "Employees" table, but we're only interested in employees who work in the "Sales" department. The `WHERE` clause filters the rows based on the condition `Department = 'Sales'`. The result is:

FirstName	LastName	Department
John	Smith	Sales
Mary	Johnson	Sales

As you can see, only employees in the "Sales" department are included in the result.

Example 2: Using Comparison Operators

sql

```sql
SELECT FirstName, LastName, Salary

FROM Employees

WHERE Salary > 50000;
```

In this example, we want to retrieve the "FirstName," "LastName," and "Salary" columns for employees with a salary greater than $50,000. We use the `>` (greater than) operator in the `WHERE` clause to specify the condition. The result includes employees who meet this salary criteria:

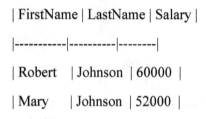

FirstName	LastName	Salary
Robert	Johnson	60000
Mary	Johnson	52000

Example 3: Using Logical Operators

sql

```sql
SELECT FirstName, LastName, Department

FROM Employees

WHERE Department = 'Sales' AND Salary > 50000;
```

In this query, we're combining multiple conditions using logical operators. We want to retrieve the "FirstName," "LastName," and "Department" columns for employees who work in the "Sales" department and have a salary greater than $50,000. The `AND` operator is used to specify both conditions. The result is:

FirstName	LastName	Department
Mary	Johnson	Sales

Only Mary Johnson meets both criteria.

Example 4: Using the OR Operator

sql

```
SELECT FirstName, LastName, Department
FROM Employees
WHERE Department = 'Sales' OR Department = 'HR';
```

In this example, we're using the `OR` operator to retrieve employees who work in either the "Sales" or "HR" department. The result includes employees from both departments:

FirstName	LastName	Department
John	Smith	Sales
Jane	Doe	HR
Mary	Johnson	Sales

Example 5: Combining AND and OR

sql

```
SELECT FirstName, LastName, Department
```

FROM Employees

WHERE (Department = 'Sales' OR Department = 'HR') AND Salary > 45000;

Here, we're using parentheses to group conditions and specify a more complex filter. We want to retrieve employees who work in either the "Sales" or "HR" department and have a salary greater than $45,000. The result is:

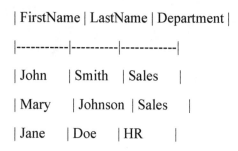

FirstName	LastName	Department
John	Smith	Sales
Mary	Johnson	Sales
Jane	Doe	HR

Example 6: Filtering with Text Patterns

sql

SELECT FirstName, LastName

FROM Employees

WHERE LastName LIKE 'S%';

In this query, we're using the `LIKE` operator to filter employees whose last names start with the letter 'S'. The `%` symbol is a wildcard that matches any number of characters. The result includes employees with last names starting with 'S':

| FirstName | LastName |

```
|-----------|----------|
| John      | Smith    |
```

Example 7: Filtering with NULL Values

sql

SELECT FirstName, LastName

FROM Employees

WHERE Department IS NULL;

In cases where you want to retrieve rows with NULL values in a specific column, you can use the `IS NULL` condition. This query retrieves employees with no assigned department:

```
| FirstName | LastName |
|-----------|----------|
| Jane      | Doe      |
```

Conclusion

The `WHERE` clause is an essential tool for filtering data in SQL queries. Whether you need to retrieve rows based on simple conditions, combine multiple criteria, or search for patterns in text data, the `WHERE` clause allows you to tailor your queries to specific requirements. As you become proficient with SQL, mastering the art of filtering data will enable you to extract valuable insights and information from your databases.

2.1.4 Sorting Data with ORDER BY

In SQL, the `ORDER BY` clause is a crucial tool for arranging the result set of your queries in a specific order. It enables you to sort your data by one or more columns, whether in ascending or descending order. Understanding how to use `ORDER BY` effectively is essential for presenting your data in a meaningful way. In this section, we will explore the usage of `ORDER BY` with practical examples and step-by-step instructions.

Understanding the ORDER BY Clause

The `ORDER BY` clause is used in SQL queries to specify the order in which rows should appear in the result set. By default, SQL returns rows in an undefined order, so using `ORDER BY` is crucial when you want to present your data in a structured manner.

Basic Usage of ORDER BY

Let's start with a simple example using a hypothetical "Products" table:

ProductID	ProductName	Price
1	Laptop	800
2	Smartphone	600
3	Tablet	400
4	Desktop	1200

Example 1: Sorting by a Single Column

sql

```sql
SELECT ProductName, Price
FROM Products
ORDER BY Price ASC;
```

In this query, we're retrieving the "ProductName" and "Price" columns from the "Products" table, and we want to sort the results by the "Price" column in ascending order (`ASC`). The result is:

ProductName	Price
Tablet	400
Smartphone	600
Laptop	800
Desktop	1200

As you can see, the result set is sorted based on the "Price" column from lowest to highest.

Example 2: Sorting in Descending Order

sql

```sql
SELECT ProductName, Price
FROM Products
ORDER BY Price DESC;
```

In this query, we're performing a similar query as in Example 1, but this time, we want to sort the results in descending order (`DESC`) based on the "Price" column. The result is:

ProductName	Price
Desktop	1200
Laptop	800
Smartphone	600
Tablet	400

The result set is now sorted from highest to lowest price.

Sorting by Multiple Columns

You can also use `ORDER BY` to sort by multiple columns. When sorting by multiple columns, SQL first sorts the data based on the first column specified and then sorts the rows with identical values in the first column based on the second column, and so on.

Example 3: Sorting by Multiple Columns

sql

SELECT ProductName, Price

FROM Products

ORDER BY Price ASC, ProductName ASC;

In this query, we're sorting the "ProductName" and "Price" columns first by "Price" in ascending order and then, within each price group, by "ProductName" in ascending order. The result is:

ProductName	Price
Tablet	400
Smartphone	600
Laptop	800
Desktop	1200

As you can see, the data is first sorted by price and then, within each price group, alphabetically by product name.

Sorting by Expressions

SQL allows you to sort data based on expressions rather than just column values. This can be useful for performing custom sorting logic. Let's say we want to sort our products based on their price range, where "Low" is below 500, "Medium" is between 500 and 1000, and "High" is above 1000:

Example 4: Sorting by Expressions

sql

```
SELECT ProductName, Price,
  CASE
    WHEN Price < 500 THEN 'Low'
    WHEN Price >= 500 AND Price <= 1000 THEN 'Medium'
```

```
    ELSE 'High'
  END AS PriceRange
FROM Products
ORDER BY
  CASE
    WHEN Price < 500 THEN 1
    WHEN Price >= 500 AND Price <= 1000 THEN 2
    ELSE 3
  END ASC, ProductName ASC;
```

In this query, we're using a `CASE` expression to categorize products into price ranges and sorting them accordingly. We first define the price range in the `SELECT` clause and then use a second `CASE` expression within the `ORDER BY` clause to specify the custom sorting order. The result is:

ProductName	Price	PriceRange
Tablet	400	Low
Smartphone	600	Medium
Laptop	800	Medium
Desktop	1200	High

The data is sorted first by the custom `PriceRange` expression and then alphabetically by product name within each price range.

Conclusion

The `ORDER BY` clause in SQL is a versatile tool for arranging your query results in a specific order. Whether you need to sort by a single column, multiple columns, or even custom expressions, `ORDER BY` allows you to present your data in a structured and meaningful way. As you continue your SQL journey, mastering the use of `ORDER BY` will enhance your ability to retrieve and present data effectively from your databases.

2.1.5 Limiting Results with LIMIT

In SQL, the `LIMIT` clause is a valuable tool for controlling the number of rows returned by a query. It allows you to retrieve a specific subset of rows from a larger result set, which can be especially useful when working with large datasets or when you only need a sample of the data. In this section, we will explore how to use the `LIMIT` clause effectively, providing practical examples and step-by-step instructions.

Understanding the LIMIT Clause

The `LIMIT` clause, as the name suggests, limits the number of rows that are returned by a SQL query. It specifies the maximum number of rows to be included in the result set. This is particularly helpful when you want to view a smaller portion of a larger dataset or when you need to implement pagination in your application.

Basic Usage of LIMIT

Let's start with a simple example using a "Customers" table:

```
| CustomerID | FirstName | LastName | Email               |
|------------|-----------|----------|---------------------|
```

1	John	Smith	john@example.com
2	Jane	Doe	jane@example.com
3	Robert	Johnson	robert@example.com
4	Mary	Johnson	mary@example.com
5	James	Brown	james@example.com

Example 1: Retrieving a Limited Number of Rows

sql

SELECT FirstName, LastName, Email

FROM Customers

LIMIT 3;

In this query, we're retrieving the "FirstName," "LastName," and "Email" columns from the "Customers" table, but we want to limit the result to only the first three rows. The `LIMIT` clause specifies the maximum number of rows to return. The result is:

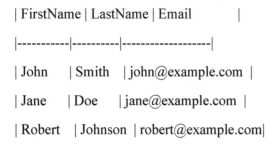

FirstName	LastName	Email
John	Smith	john@example.com
Jane	Doe	jane@example.com
Robert	Johnson	robert@example.com

As you can see, the result set contains only the first three rows from the "Customers" table.

Example 2: Using LIMIT with OFFSET (Pagination)

sql

SELECT FirstName, LastName, Email

FROM Customers

LIMIT 3 OFFSET 2;

In this example, we're still interested in the "FirstName," "LastName," and "Email" columns from the "Customers" table, but this time we want to retrieve a specific page of results. The `LIMIT` clause limits the number of rows returned to three, and the `OFFSET` clause specifies the starting point for the limit. In this case, we start at row 2. The result is:

FirstName	LastName	Email
Robert	Johnson	robert@example.com
Mary	Johnson	mary@example.com
James	Brown	james@example.com

This allows you to implement pagination for displaying data in chunks.

Using LIMIT with ORDER BY

`LIMIT` is often used in combination with the `ORDER BY` clause to retrieve a specific number of rows based on a specified sorting order.

Example 3: Using LIMIT with ORDER BY

```sql
SELECT FirstName, LastName, Email
FROM Customers
ORDER BY LastName ASC
LIMIT 2;
```

In this query, we're retrieving the "FirstName," "LastName," and "Email" columns from the "Customers" table. We want to sort the results by the "LastName" column in ascending order and limit the result to the first two rows. The result is:

FirstName	LastName	Email
Jane	Doe	jane@example.com
James	Brown	james@example.com

The data is sorted by last name, and we retrieve the top two records.

Limiting Results for Subqueries

The `LIMIT` clause can also be used within subqueries to restrict the number of rows returned within a subquery.

Example 4: Using LIMIT in Subqueries

sql

SELECT FirstName, LastName, Email

```
FROM Customers

WHERE CustomerID IN (

 SELECT CustomerID

 FROM Orders

 WHERE TotalAmount > 1000

 LIMIT 2

);
```

In this example, we're retrieving customer information from the "Customers" table for customers who have placed orders with a total amount greater than 1000. The subquery retrieves the first two customer IDs meeting this condition using `LIMIT`, and then the main query retrieves customer details for those IDs. This can be helpful when you want to limit the result of a subquery to a manageable number of rows.

Conclusion

The `LIMIT` clause in SQL is a powerful tool for controlling the number of rows returned by a query. Whether you need to retrieve a specific subset of data, implement pagination, or restrict the result of a subquery, `LIMIT` allows you to tailor your query results to your specific requirements. As you continue to work with SQL and handle datasets of varying sizes, mastering the use of `LIMIT` will be essential for efficient data retrieval and presentation.

2.2 The INSERT Statement: Adding New Data

2.2.1 Inserting Data into Tables

In SQL, the `INSERT` statement is used to add new data into tables. It is a fundamental operation for creating records within a database. Whether you're adding a single row or multiple rows at once, understanding how to use the `INSERT` statement effectively is essential. In this section, we will explore the usage of the `INSERT` statement with practical examples and step-by-step instructions.

Understanding the INSERT Statement

The `INSERT` statement is one of the core SQL statements used for data manipulation. It allows you to add new rows of data into an existing table. When using `INSERT`, you specify the target table and provide the values that should be inserted into each column of the table.

Basic Usage of INSERT

Let's start with a simple example using a hypothetical "Employees" table:

EmployeeID	FirstName	LastName	Department	Salary
1	John	Smith	Sales	50000
2	Jane	Doe	HR	45000
3	Robert	Johnson	IT	60000

Example 1: Inserting a Single Row

sql

```sql
INSERT INTO Employees (FirstName, LastName, Department, Salary)
VALUES ('Mary', 'Wilson', 'Marketing', 55000);
```

In this query, we're adding a new employee, Mary Wilson, to the "Employees" table. We specify the target table after `INSERT INTO` and provide the values to be inserted into the columns listed in parentheses. The result is:

EmployeeID	FirstName	LastName	Department	Salary
1	John	Smith	Sales	50000
2	Jane	Doe	HR	45000
3	Robert	Johnson	IT	60000
4	Mary	Wilson	Marketing	55000

As you can see, a new row has been added to the table with the values provided.

Example 2: Inserting Multiple Rows

sql

```sql
INSERT INTO Employees (FirstName, LastName, Department, Salary)
VALUES
  ('David', 'Brown', 'Finance', 58000),
  ('Laura', 'Anderson', 'Sales', 52000);
```

In this example, we're inserting two new employees, David Brown and Laura Anderson, into the "Employees" table. We specify multiple sets of values within the `VALUES` clause to insert multiple rows in a single `INSERT` statement. The result is:

EmployeeID	FirstName	LastName	Department	Salary
1	John	Smith	Sales	50000
2	Jane	Doe	HR	45000
3	Robert	Johnson	IT	60000
4	Mary	Wilson	Marketing	55000
5	David	Brown	Finance	58000
6	Laura	Anderson	Sales	52000

The table now contains two additional rows for David Brown and Laura Anderson.

Inserting Data into Specific Columns

You can also insert data into specific columns of a table, especially when you don't need to provide values for all columns.

Example 3: Inserting Data into Specific Columns

sql

INSERT INTO Employees (FirstName, LastName)

VALUES ('Steven', 'Williams');

In this query, we're inserting a new employee, Steven Williams, into the "Employees" table. However, we only provide values for the "FirstName" and "LastName" columns, leaving the "Department" and "Salary" columns empty. The result is:

EmployeeID	FirstName	LastName	Department	Salary
1	John	Smith	Sales	50000
2	Jane	Doe	HR	45000
3	Robert	Johnson	IT	60000
4	Mary	Wilson	Marketing	55000
5	David	Brown	Finance	58000
6	Laura	Anderson	Sales	52000
7	Steven	Williams		

As you can see, the new row contains values only for "FirstName" and "LastName," and the other columns are left empty.

Inserting Data from Another Table

The `INSERT` statement can also be used to copy data from one table into another. This is useful for duplicating or archiving data.

Example 4: Inserting Data from Another Table

sql

INSERT INTO ArchivedEmployees (EmployeeID, FirstName, LastName, Department, Salary)

SELECT EmployeeID, FirstName, LastName, Department, Salary

```sql
FROM Employees
WHERE Department = 'HR';
```

In this query, we're inserting data from the "Employees" table into an "ArchivedEmployees" table, but only for employees in the HR department. We use a `SELECT` statement to specify which data to copy. The result is:

(Contents of "ArchivedEmployees" table)

EmployeeID	FirstName	LastName	Department	Salary
2	Jane	Doe	HR	45000

This query creates a copy of the HR department's data in the "ArchivedEmployees" table.

Handling Auto-Increment Columns

In many databases, it's common to have auto-increment columns, often used for primary keys. When inserting data into a table with auto-increment columns, you don't need to specify a value for that column. The database system will automatically assign a unique value.

Example 5: Inserting Data into a Table with Auto-Increment

sql

```sql
INSERT INTO Orders (CustomerID, OrderDate, TotalAmount)
VALUES (3, '2023-09-15', 1200.00);
```

In this query, we're inserting a new order into the

"Orders" table. The "OrderID" column is an auto-increment primary key, so we don't need to provide a value for it. The database system will assign a unique "OrderID" value automatically. The result is:

OrderID	CustomerID	OrderDate	TotalAmount
1	3	2023-09-15	1200.00

The "OrderID" column was assigned the value 1 automatically.

Conclusion

The `INSERT` statement in SQL is a fundamental operation for adding new data to tables. Whether you're inserting a single row or multiple rows, specifying values for specific columns or copying data from another table, understanding how to use `INSERT` effectively is essential for managing your database's data. As you continue to work with SQL, you'll frequently encounter situations where the `INSERT` statement is a valuable tool for maintaining and updating your database records.

2.2.2 Using INSERT SELECT

In SQL, the `INSERT INTO...SELECT` statement is a powerful tool that allows you to insert data into a table based on the result of a `SELECT` query. This feature provides a flexible way to copy data from one table into another, generate new records, and perform complex data manipulations. In this section, we will explore the usage of the `INSERT INTO...SELECT` statement with practical examples and step-by-step instructions.

Understanding the INSERT INTO...SELECT Statement

The `INSERT INTO...SELECT` statement combines two SQL operations: inserting data into a table (`INSERT INTO`) and retrieving data from one or more tables using a `SELECT` query. This combination enables you to insert specific data or calculated results into a target table based on the conditions defined in the `SELECT` query.

Basic Usage of INSERT INTO...SELECT

Let's start with a simple example using two hypothetical tables, "Employees" and "Department":

Employees Table:

EmployeeID	FirstName	LastName	DepartmentID	Salary
1	John	Smith	101	50000
2	Jane	Doe	102	45000
3	Robert	Johnson	101	60000

Department Table:

DepartmentID	DepartmentName
101	Sales
102	HR
103	Marketing

Example 1: Inserting Data into a New Table

sql

CREATE TABLE SalesEmployees AS

SELECT EmployeeID, FirstName, LastName, Salary

FROM Employees

WHERE DepartmentID = 101;

In this query, we're creating a new table called "SalesEmployees" and inserting data into it. We specify the columns we want to insert (EmployeeID, FirstName, LastName, and Salary) by using a `SELECT` query. The `SELECT` query retrieves employee records where the "DepartmentID" is 101 (Sales department). The result is:

SalesEmployees Table:

EmployeeID	FirstName	LastName	Salary
1	John	Smith	50000
3	Robert	Johnson	60000

As you can see, the "SalesEmployees" table now contains data only for employees in the Sales department.

Example 2: Inserting Data into an Existing Table

sql

INSERT INTO Department (DepartmentName)

SELECT 'Logistics'

UNION

SELECT 'Finance';

In this query, we're inserting two new department names, 'Logistics' and 'Finance,' into the existing "Department" table. We use the `INSERT INTO` statement and combine it with a `SELECT` query that specifies the values to be inserted. The `UNION` operator combines the results of two `SELECT` queries into a single list. The result is:

Department Table:

DepartmentID	DepartmentName
101	Sales
102	HR
103	Marketing
104	Logistics
105	Finance

The "Department" table has been updated with two new departments.

Copying Data Between Tables

The `INSERT INTO...SELECT` statement is commonly used to copy data from one table to another. Let's consider an example where we want to copy all employees from the "Employees" table to a new table called "AllEmployees":

Example 3: Copying Data Between Tables

sql

```
CREATE TABLE AllEmployees AS

SELECT *

FROM Employees;
```

In this query, we create a new table "AllEmployees" and insert all records from the "Employees" table into it. The `SELECT *` query retrieves all columns and rows from the "Employees" table. The result is a new table that is an exact copy of the "Employees" table.

Performing Calculations During Insertion

You can also perform calculations and transformations on the data while inserting it into a target table. Let's say we want to create a new table called "HighEarners" to store employees who earn more than $55,000:

Example 4: Inserting Data with Calculations

sql

```
CREATE TABLE HighEarners AS

SELECT EmployeeID, FirstName, LastName, Salary, Salary * 12 AS AnnualIncome

FROM Employees

WHERE Salary > 55000;
```

In this query, we create a new table "HighEarners" and insert data into it. The `SELECT` query calculates the annual income by multiplying the monthly salary (`Salary`) by 12. We only insert records where the salary is greater than $55,000. The result is:

HighEarners Table:

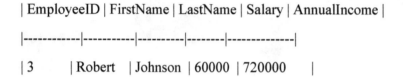

EmployeeID	FirstName	LastName	Salary	AnnualIncome
3	Robert	Johnson	60000	720000

The "HighEarners" table contains data for employees with an annual income greater than $55,000.

Conclusion

The `INSERT INTO...SELECT` statement in SQL is a versatile tool for inserting data into tables based on the results of `SELECT` queries. Whether you need to create new tables, copy data between tables, or perform calculations during insertion, this feature provides you with the flexibility to manipulate and manage your data effectively. As you continue to work with SQL, you'll find that the `INSERT INTO...SELECT` statement is a valuable asset for handling various data manipulation tasks within your database.

2.2.3 Handling Errors when Inserting Data

When working with SQL and the `INSERT` statement to add new data to tables, it's essential to consider error handling. Errors can occur for various reasons, such as data type mismatches, constraint violations, or duplicate key values. In this section, we will explore how to handle errors effectively when inserting data into tables, providing practical examples and step-by-step instructions.

Understanding Errors in SQL

Before diving into error handling techniques, it's crucial to understand the types of errors that can occur during data insertion:

1. **Data Type Mismatch**: When you try to insert data with incompatible data types into a column, such as inserting a string into an integer column.

2. **Constraint Violations:** Constraints, such as unique constraints or foreign key constraints, can be violated if the inserted data doesn't meet the specified criteria.

3. **Duplicate Key Values:** If you attempt to insert a record with a primary key value that already exists in the table, it will result in a duplicate key error.

4. **Data Length Exceeds Column Size:** If the length of the data being inserted exceeds the defined column size, it can lead to truncation or data loss.

Handling Errors Using SQL's Error Codes

SQL provides error codes that can help you identify the type of error that occurred. These error codes can be used in your SQL statements to handle errors gracefully. The SQL standard defines error codes and their meanings, allowing you to create conditional logic to respond to specific errors.

Example 1: Handling Data Type Mismatch Errors

Let's consider a scenario where you're inserting data into an "Employees" table, and you mistakenly provide a non-integer value for the "EmployeeID" column, which is of data type integer.

```sql
INSERT INTO Employees (EmployeeID, FirstName, LastName)
VALUES ('A123', 'John', 'Doe');
```

In this case, the data type of 'A123' doesn't match the integer data type of the "EmployeeID" column. As a result, you might encounter an error with an error code, such as SQL State '22018' (data exception - invalid character value for cast).

To handle this error, you can use a `TRY...CATCH` block or a similar error handling mechanism provided by your SQL database system. Here's an example using SQL Server's `TRY...CATCH` block:

```sql
BEGIN TRY
    INSERT INTO Employees (EmployeeID, FirstName, LastName)
    VALUES ('A123', 'John', 'Doe');
END TRY
BEGIN CATCH
    PRINT 'An error occurred: ' + ERROR_MESSAGE();
```

END CATCH;

This code attempts to insert the data and, if an error occurs, captures the error message using `ERROR_MESSAGE()`. You can then take appropriate action, such as logging the error or notifying users.

Example 2: Handling Constraint Violation Errors

Suppose you have a "Students" table with a unique constraint on the "StudentID" column to ensure that each student has a unique identifier. If you attempt to insert a new student with a duplicate "StudentID," it will violate the unique constraint.

sql

INSERT INTO Students (StudentID, FirstName, LastName)

VALUES (101, 'Alice', 'Johnson');

In this case, if the StudentID 101 already exists in the table, you might encounter an error with an error code like SQL State '23505' (unique violation).

To handle this error, you can use error checking within your SQL statements or leverage database-specific error handling mechanisms. Here's an example using PostgreSQL's `ON CONFLICT` clause:

sql

INSERT INTO Students (StudentID, FirstName, LastName)

```sql
VALUES (101, 'Alice', 'Johnson')
ON CONFLICT (StudentID) DO NOTHING;
```

In this example, the `ON CONFLICT` clause allows you to specify what action to take when a conflict (duplicate key) occurs. Using `DO NOTHING` ensures that the insertion is skipped if a conflict arises.

Example 3: Handling Duplicate Key Errors

Handling duplicate key errors often involves checking whether the key already exists before attempting an insertion. You can use conditional statements to achieve this.

sql

```sql
DECLARE @StudentID INT = 101;

IF NOT EXISTS (SELECT 1 FROM Students WHERE StudentID = @StudentID)
BEGIN
    INSERT INTO Students (StudentID, FirstName, LastName)
    VALUES (@StudentID, 'Alice', 'Johnson');
END
ELSE
BEGIN
    PRINT 'Student with StudentID ' + CAST(@StudentID AS VARCHAR) + ' already exists.';
END
```

In this SQL Server example, we first check whether a student with the same StudentID exists in the "Students" table. If not, we proceed with the insertion. If a duplicate is detected, we print an error message.

Handling Errors Using Database-Specific Functions

Database systems often provide functions or procedures for handling errors. For example, in SQL Server, you can use the `TRY...CATCH` block as demonstrated earlier. In PostgreSQL, you can use `BEGIN...EXCEPTION` blocks.

Example 4: Handling Errors in PostgreSQL

sql

```sql
BEGIN;
    INSERT INTO Students (StudentID, FirstName, LastName)
    VALUES (101, 'Alice', 'Johnson');
EXCEPTION
    WHEN unique_violation THEN
        RAISE NOTICE 'Student with StudentID 101 already exists.';
ROLLBACK;
```

In this PostgreSQL example, we begin a transaction with `BEGIN`, attempt the insertion, and handle the unique violation error with an `EXCEPTION` block. We raise a notice and then roll back the transaction to ensure that the insertion doesn't take place.

Conclusion

Handling errors when inserting data into SQL tables is an important aspect of database management. SQL provides error codes and mechanisms for identifying and responding to different types of errors, such as data type mismatches, constraint violations, and duplicate key errors. By understanding these errors and using appropriate error handling techniques, you can ensure data integrity and create robust database applications that gracefully handle unexpected situations. Always refer to your database system's documentation for specific error codes and error handling features available in your environment.

2.3 The UPDATE Statement: Modifying Data

2.3.1 Updating Data in Tables

The `UPDATE` statement in SQL is a powerful tool that allows you to modify existing data in tables. Whether you need to change a single value or update multiple records, understanding how to use the `UPDATE` statement effectively is essential for maintaining and managing your database. In this section, we will explore the usage of the `UPDATE` statement with practical examples and step-by-step instructions.

Understanding the UPDATE Statement

The `UPDATE` statement is used to modify existing records in a table. It allows you to change the values of one or more columns for specific rows that meet a certain condition. When using `UPDATE`, you specify the target table, the columns to be updated, the new values, and the condition that determines which rows should be updated.

Basic Usage of UPDATE

Let's start with a simple example using a hypothetical "Employees" table:

Employees Table:

EmployeeID	FirstName	LastName	Department	Salary
1	John	Smith	Sales	50000
2	Jane	Doe	HR	45000
3	Robert	Johnson	IT	60000

| 4 | Mary | Wilson | Marketing | 55000 |

Example 1: Updating a Single Value

sql

UPDATE Employees

SET Salary = 52000

WHERE EmployeeID = 2;

In this query, we're updating the "Salary" column for the employee with "EmployeeID" 2 (Jane Doe). We use the `SET` clause to specify the column to be updated and its new value. The `WHERE` clause determines which row(s) will be updated. After executing this query, Jane's salary is changed to $52,000.

Employees Table After Update:

EmployeeID	FirstName	LastName	Department	Salary
1	John	Smith	Sales	50000
2	Jane	Doe	HR	52000
3	Robert	Johnson	IT	60000
4	Mary	Wilson	Marketing	55000

Example 2: Updating Multiple Columns

sql

UPDATE Employees

SET Salary = 61000, Department = 'Finance'

WHERE EmployeeID = 3;

In this query, we're updating both the "Salary" and "Department" columns for the employee with "EmployeeID" 3 (Robert Johnson). The `SET` clause allows us to specify multiple columns to be updated with their new values. After executing this query, Robert's salary is changed to $61,000, and his department is updated to "Finance."

Employees Table After Update:

EmployeeID	FirstName	LastName	Department	Salary
1	John	Smith	Sales	50000
2	Jane	Doe	HR	52000
3	Robert	Johnson	Finance	61000
4	Mary	Wilson	Marketing	55000

Example 3: Updating Multiple Rows

sql

UPDATE Employees

SET Salary = Salary * 1.05

WHERE Department = 'Sales';

In this query, we're updating the "Salary" for all employees in the "Sales" department. We use the `SET` clause to multiply the current salary by 1.05 (a 5% increase). The `WHERE` clause ensures that the update only applies to rows in the "Sales" department. After executing this query, all sales department employees receive a 5% salary increase.

Employees Table After Update:

EmployeeID	FirstName	LastName	Department	Salary
1	John	Smith	Sales	52500
2	Jane	Doe	HR	52000
3	Robert	Johnson	Finance	61000
4	Mary	Wilson	Marketing	55000

Updating Data Based on Conditions

One of the key features of the `UPDATE` statement is the ability to update data based on specific conditions. The `WHERE` clause plays a crucial role in determining which rows are affected by the update.

Example 4: Updating Data Based on a Condition

sql

```
UPDATE Employees
SET Department = 'Logistics'
WHERE EmployeeID > 2 AND Salary < 60000;
```

In this query, we're updating the "Department" column for employees who meet two conditions: their "EmployeeID" is greater than 2, and their "Salary" is less than $60,000. Only employees who satisfy both conditions will have their department changed to "Logistics."

Employees Table After Update:

EmployeeID	FirstName	LastName	Department	Salary
1	John	Smith	Sales	52500
2	Jane	Doe	HR	52000
3	Robert	Johnson	Logistics	61000
4	Mary	Wilson	Logistics	55000

Updating Data Safely

When updating data, especially in production databases, it's essential to consider safety measures to prevent unintended data modifications. Here are some best practices:

1. Backup Data: Before making significant updates, perform a backup of the data to restore it in case of unexpected issues.

2. Use Transactions: Wrap your `UPDATE` statement in a transaction to ensure that the changes are applied atomically and can be rolled back if needed.

3. Test in a Sandbox: Test your `UPDATE` statements in a non-production environment or sandbox to verify their accuracy and impact.

4. Check Affected Rows: After running an `UPDATE` statement, check the number of rows affected to ensure it matches your expectations.

Conclusion

The `UPDATE` statement is a fundamental SQL operation for modifying existing data in tables. Whether you need to update a single value, multiple columns, or multiple rows based on specific conditions, understanding how to use the `UPDATE` statement effectively is crucial for maintaining data integrity and managing your database. By following best practices and testing your updates in a safe environment, you can confidently use the `UPDATE` statement to make changes to your database while minimizing the risk of unintended consequences.

2.3.2 Using UPDATE with WHERE

The `UPDATE` statement in SQL allows you to modify data in a table, but often, you don't want to update every row in a table. The `WHERE` clause in combination with the `UPDATE` statement provides a way to selectively update rows that meet specific conditions. In this section, we will explore how to use the `UPDATE` statement with the `WHERE` clause to precisely modify data in tables, providing practical examples and step-by-step instructions.

Understanding the UPDATE Statement with WHERE

The `UPDATE` statement with a `WHERE` clause is used to selectively update rows in a table based on specified conditions. It allows you to control which rows are modified, ensuring that only the desired data is changed.

Basic Usage of UPDATE with WHERE

Let's start with a simple example using a hypothetical "Products" table:

Products Table:

ProductID	ProductName	Category	Price
1	Laptop	Electronics	800
2	Smartphone	Electronics	500
3	Desk	Furniture	150
4	Chair	Furniture	75
5	Microwave	Appliances	200

Example 1: Updating Data with WHERE

sql

```
UPDATE Products
SET Price = 850
WHERE ProductName = 'Laptop';
```

In this query, we're updating the "Price" of the product with the "ProductName" 'Laptop' to $850. The `SET` clause specifies the column to be updated and its new value, and the `WHERE` clause ensures that only rows where the "ProductName" is 'Laptop' are affected.

Products Table After Update:

ProductID	ProductName	Category	Price

1	Laptop	Electronics	850
2	Smartphone	Electronics	500
3	Desk	Furniture	150
4	Chair	Furniture	75
5	Microwave	Appliances	200

As a result of this update, only the laptop's price has changed.

Example 2: Updating Multiple Rows with WHERE

sql

UPDATE Products

SET Price = Price * 1.1

WHERE Category = 'Furniture';

In this query, we're updating the "Price" of all products in the 'Furniture' category by increasing their prices by 10% (multiplying the current price by 1.1). The `SET` clause specifies the column to be updated, and the `WHERE` clause filters rows where the "Category" is 'Furniture.'

Products Table After Update:

ProductID	ProductName	Category	Price
1	Laptop	Electronics	850
2	Smartphone	Electronics	500

| 3 | Desk | Furniture | 165 |

| 4 | Chair | Furniture | 82.5 |

| 5 | Microwave | Appliances | 200 |

As a result, all products in the 'Furniture' category have had their prices updated.

Example 3: Updating Data Based on Multiple Conditions

sql

UPDATE Products

SET Price = 700

WHERE Category = 'Electronics' AND Price > 700;

In this query, we're updating the "Price" of products in the 'Electronics' category that currently have a price greater than $700. The `SET` clause specifies the new price, and the `WHERE` clause combines two conditions using the `AND` operator. Only products meeting both conditions will be updated.

Products Table After Update:

ProductID	ProductName	Category	Price
1	Laptop	Electronics	700
2	Smartphone	Electronics	500
3	Desk	Furniture	165
4	Chair	Furniture	82.5

| 5 | Microwave | Appliances | 200 |

In this case, only the 'Laptop' had its price updated because it was the only product in the 'Electronics' category with a price greater than $700.

Updating Data Safely with WHERE

When using the `UPDATE` statement with the `WHERE` clause, it's crucial to ensure that the conditions you specify are accurate to avoid unintended updates. Here are some best practices:

1. Test Conditions: Before executing an `UPDATE` statement, run a `SELECT` query with the same conditions to verify which rows will be affected.

2. Use Transactions: Wrap your `UPDATE` statement in a transaction to ensure that the changes are applied atomically and can be rolled back if needed.

3. Backup Data: Before making significant updates, perform a backup of the data to restore it in case of unexpected issues.

Conclusion

The `UPDATE` statement with the `WHERE` clause is a powerful SQL operation for selectively modifying data in tables. By specifying conditions in the `WHERE` clause, you can control which rows are updated, ensuring that your updates are precise and targeted. When used carefully and in conjunction with best practices, the `UPDATE` statement with `WHERE` allows you to safely and effectively make changes to your database's data.

2.4 The DELETE Statement: Removing Data

2.4.1 Deleting Data from Tables

The `DELETE` statement in SQL is used to remove data from tables. It provides a way to selectively delete one or more rows based on specified conditions. In this section, we will explore how to use the `DELETE` statement effectively to remove data from tables, providing practical examples and step-by-step instructions.

Understanding the DELETE Statement

The `DELETE` statement is used to remove one or more rows from a table. It allows you to specify conditions in a `WHERE` clause to determine which rows should be deleted. Be cautious when using the `DELETE` statement, as it permanently removes data from the table.

Basic Usage of DELETE

Let's start with a simple example using a hypothetical "Customers" table:

Customers Table:

CustomerID	FirstName	LastName	Email
1	John	Smith	john@example.com
2	Jane	Doe	jane@example.com
3	Robert	Johnson	robert@example.com
4	Mary	Wilson	mary@example.com

| 5 | David | Brown | david@example.com |

Example 1: Deleting a Single Row

sql

DELETE FROM Customers

WHERE CustomerID = 3;

In this query, we're deleting a single row from the "Customers" table where the "CustomerID" is 3 (Robert Johnson). The `DELETE FROM` statement specifies the target table, and the `WHERE` clause specifies the condition for deletion. After executing this query, Robert's record is permanently removed from the table.

Customers Table After Delete:

CustomerID	FirstName	LastName	Email
1	John	Smith	john@example.com
2	Jane	Doe	jane@example.com
4	Mary	Wilson	mary@example.com
5	David	Brown	david@example.com

Example 2: Deleting Multiple Rows

sql

DELETE FROM Customers

WHERE LastName = 'Doe';

In this query, we're deleting multiple rows from the "Customers" table where the "LastName" is 'Doe' (Jane Doe). The `DELETE FROM` statement, along with the `WHERE` clause, allows us to delete all records that meet the specified condition. After executing this query, both Jane and John Doe's records are removed from the table.

Customers Table After Delete:

CustomerID	FirstName	LastName	Email
4	Mary	Wilson	mary@example.com
5	David	Brown	david@example.com

Example 3: Deleting All Rows

sql

DELETE FROM Customers;

In this query, we're deleting all rows from the "Customers" table without specifying a `WHERE` clause. As a result, all records in the table are permanently deleted. Be extremely cautious when using this approach, as it erases all data in the table.

Customers Table After Delete:

The "Customers" table will be empty after executing this query.

Deleting Data Based on Conditions

The real power of the `DELETE` statement lies in its ability to delete data based on specified conditions using the `WHERE` clause.

Example 4: Deleting Data Based on a Condition

sql

DELETE FROM Customers

WHERE Email IS NULL;

In this query, we're deleting rows from the "Customers" table where the "Email" column is NULL. The `DELETE FROM` statement, combined with the `WHERE` clause, allows us to remove records that don't have an email address. After executing this query, any customer without an email address will be removed from the table.

Customers Table After Delete:

CustomerID	FirstName	LastName	Email
4	Mary	Wilson	mary@example.com
5	David	Brown	david@example.com

Deleting Data Safely

When using the `DELETE` statement, it's crucial to ensure that the conditions you specify are accurate to avoid unintended data removal. Here are some best practices:

1. Test Conditions: Before executing a `DELETE` statement, run a `SELECT` query with the same conditions to verify which rows will be affected.

2. Use Transactions: Wrap your `DELETE` statement in a transaction to ensure that the changes are applied atomically and can be rolled back if needed.

3. Backup Data: Before making significant deletions, perform a backup of the data to restore it in case of unexpected issues.

Conclusion

The `DELETE` statement in SQL provides a way to remove data from tables based on specified conditions. By using the `DELETE` statement effectively, you can precisely remove unwanted data while keeping your database clean and organized. However, be cautious when using the `DELETE` statement, as it permanently erases data. Always verify conditions and consider safety measures to prevent unintended data removal.

2.4.2 Using DELETE with WHERE

The `DELETE` statement in SQL allows you to remove data from tables selectively, based on specified conditions. When combined with the `WHERE` clause, it becomes a powerful tool for precise data deletion. In this section, we will explore how to use the `DELETE` statement with the `WHERE` clause effectively, providing practical examples and step-by-step instructions.

Understanding DELETE with WHERE

The `DELETE` statement with the `WHERE` clause is used to selectively delete rows from a table based on specified conditions. It gives you control over which rows are removed, ensuring that only the desired data is deleted while preserving other records.

Basic Usage of DELETE with WHERE

Let's start with a simple example using a hypothetical "Orders" table:

Orders Table:

OrderID	CustomerID	OrderDate	Status
1	101	2023-01-15	Shipped
2	102	2023-02-10	Pending
3	101	2023-03-05	Delivered
4	103	2023-04-20	Shipped
5	102	2023-05-12	Pending

Example 1: Deleting Rows with WHERE

sql

DELETE FROM Orders

WHERE Status = 'Delivered';

In this query, we're deleting rows from the "Orders" table where the "Status" is 'Delivered'. The `DELETE FROM` statement specifies the target table, and the `WHERE` clause determines the condition for deletion. After executing this query, all orders with a 'Delivered' status are permanently removed from the table.

Orders Table After Delete:

OrderID	CustomerID	OrderDate	Status
1	101	2023-01-15	Shipped
2	102	2023-02-10	Pending
4	103	2023-04-20	Shipped
5	102	2023-05-12	Pending

As a result of this operation, all orders with a 'Delivered' status have been removed.

Example 2: Deleting Rows Based on Multiple Conditions

sql

DELETE FROM Orders

WHERE CustomerID = 102 AND Status = 'Pending';

In this query, we're deleting rows from the "Orders" table where the "CustomerID" is 102 and the "Status" is 'Pending'. The `DELETE FROM` statement, along with the `WHERE` clause, allows us to remove specific orders based on two conditions. After executing this query, only the orders that meet both conditions are deleted.

Orders Table After Delete:

OrderID	CustomerID	OrderDate	Status
1	101	2023-01-15	Shipped
4	103	2023-04-20	Shipped

In this case, only the order placed by CustomerID 102 with a 'Pending' status has been deleted.

Example 3: Deleting Rows with Date Condition

sql

DELETE FROM Orders

WHERE OrderDate < '2023-04-01';

In this query, we're deleting rows from the "Orders" table where the "OrderDate" is before April 1, 2023. The `DELETE FROM` statement, along with the `WHERE` clause, enables us to remove orders based on a date condition. After executing this query, all orders placed before April 1, 2023, are removed.

Orders Table After Delete:

OrderID	CustomerID	OrderDate	Status
4	103	2023-04-20	Shipped
5	102	2023-05-12	Pending

As a result, orders placed before April 1, 2023, have been deleted.

Deleting Data Safely with WHERE

Using the `DELETE` statement with the `WHERE` clause requires careful consideration to avoid unintentional data deletion. Here are some best practices:

1. Test Conditions: Before executing a `DELETE` statement, run a `SELECT` query with the same conditions to verify which rows will be affected.

2. Use Transactions: Wrap your `DELETE` statement in a transaction to ensure that the changes are applied atomically and can be rolled back if needed.

3. Backup Data: Before making significant deletions, perform a backup of the data to restore it in case of unexpected issues.

Conclusion

The `DELETE` statement with the `WHERE` clause is a valuable SQL operation for selectively removing data from tables. By specifying conditions in the `WHERE` clause, you can precisely delete the desired data while preserving other records. It is essential to use this statement carefully and consider safety measures to prevent unintended data deletion, ensuring the integrity of your database.

PART III
Creating and Managing Tables

3.1 Creating New Tables with CREATE TABLE

3.1.1. Defining Data Types for Columns

In the world of SQL, creating new tables is a fundamental skill. Tables are the building blocks of a relational database, and understanding how to define columns and their data types is crucial. In this section, we will explore the `CREATE TABLE` statement, focusing on how to define data types for columns.

Understanding CREATE TABLE

The `CREATE TABLE` statement in SQL is used to create a new table in a database. It allows you to specify the table's structure by defining columns, their names, and data types. Data types define the kind of data that can be stored in a column, such as text, numbers, dates, or binary data.

Basic Syntax of CREATE TABLE

Here is the basic syntax for creating a new table:

sql

```
CREATE TABLE table_name (
    column1_name data_type,
```

```
    column2_name data_type,

    ...

);
```

Let's dive into the details of defining data types for columns.

Common Data Types

SQL supports various data types to cover a wide range of data. Here are some common data types:

1. INTEGER or INT: Used for whole numbers.

2. VARCHAR(n): Variable-length character strings with a maximum length of 'n'.

3. CHAR(n): Fixed-length character strings with a length of 'n'.

4. FLOAT: Used for floating-point numbers.

5. DATE: Represents a date (year, month, day).

6. TIME: Represents a time of day (hour, minute, second).

7. DATETIME: Represents both date and time.

8. BOOLEAN: Represents true or false values.

Defining Columns with Data Types

Let's create a new table called "Employees" with several columns and define their data types:

sql

```sql
CREATE TABLE Employees (
    EmployeeID INT,
    FirstName VARCHAR(50),
    LastName VARCHAR(50),
    BirthDate DATE,
    Salary FLOAT,
    Active BOOLEAN
);
```

In this example, we've created a table named "Employees" with the following columns:

- `EmployeeID`: An integer that will store employee IDs.

- `FirstName` and `LastName`: Variable-length character strings that will store employee names.

- `BirthDate`: A date data type to store employee birthdates.

- `Salary`: A floating-point number to store employee salaries.

- `Active`: A boolean data type to indicate whether an employee is active or not.

Adding Constraints

In addition to data types, you can add constraints to columns to enforce rules and maintain data integrity. Common constraints include:

- **PRIMARY KEY**: Ensures each row in a table is unique and identifies it uniquely.

- **NOT NULL**: Ensures that a column cannot have NULL (empty) values.

- **UNIQUE:** Ensures that all values in a column are unique.

- **DEFAULT:** Provides a default value for a column when no value is specified during insertion.

Here's an example of creating a table with constraints:

sql

```sql
CREATE TABLE Customers (
    CustomerID INT PRIMARY KEY,
    FirstName VARCHAR(50) NOT NULL,
    LastName VARCHAR(50) NOT NULL,
    Email VARCHAR(100) UNIQUE,
    RegistrationDate DATE DEFAULT CURRENT_DATE
);
```

In this table:

- `CustomerID` is the primary key, ensuring each customer has a unique ID.

- `FirstName` and `LastName` cannot be NULL, ensuring that customer names are always provided.

- `Email` must be unique, preventing duplicate email addresses.

- `RegistrationDate` has a default value of the current date, so if no registration date is specified during insertion, the current date is used.

Creating Tables with Relationships

In a relational database, tables often have relationships with each other. This is achieved by defining foreign keys that reference the primary key of another table. Let's create two tables, "Orders" and "Customers," with a relationship:

sql

```sql
CREATE TABLE Customers (

    CustomerID INT PRIMARY KEY,

    FirstName VARCHAR(50),

    LastName VARCHAR(50)

);


CREATE TABLE Orders (

    OrderID INT PRIMARY KEY,

    CustomerID INT,

    OrderDate DATE,

    FOREIGN KEY (CustomerID) REFERENCES Customers(CustomerID)

);
```

In this example:

- The "Customers" table has a primary key on `CustomerID`.

- The "Orders" table has a foreign key on `CustomerID`, which references the `CustomerID` column in the "Customers" table. This establishes a relationship between the two tables.

Creating Tables in Specific Databases

In most database systems, you can create tables in specific databases. This is useful when you're working with multiple databases within the same database management system. Here's how to create a table in a specific database:

```sql
CREATE TABLE mydb.Employees (
    EmployeeID INT,
    FirstName VARCHAR(50),
    LastName VARCHAR(50)
);
```

In this example, we're creating the "Employees" table in the "mydb" database.

Conclusion

Creating tables with the `CREATE TABLE` statement is a fundamental skill in SQL. Understanding how to define columns, their data types, and constraints is essential for designing a well-structured database. Additionally, defining relationships between tables using foreign keys enables you to create robust relational databases. By mastering these concepts, you can efficiently create and manage tables to store and organize your data.

3.1.2. Setting Data Constraints

In the world of database management, maintaining data integrity is of paramount importance. Data constraints are rules that define the characteristics and properties of data stored in a table, ensuring that it remains accurate, consistent, and reliable. In this section, we will delve into the art of setting data constraints using the `CREATE TABLE` statement.

Understanding Data Constraints

Data constraints are rules applied to columns within a table. They help enforce business rules and prevent the entry of invalid or inconsistent data into the database. Common data constraints include:

1. PRIMARY KEY: Ensures each row in a table is unique and identifies it uniquely. A table can have only one primary key.

2. UNIQUE: Ensures that all values in a column are unique across rows in the table.

3. NOT NULL: Requires that a column must always contain a value and cannot be left empty (NULL).

4. DEFAULT: Specifies a default value for a column when no value is provided during insertion.

5. CHECK: Defines a condition that values in a column must meet. If the condition is not met, the data insertion or update is rejected.

Defining Constraints with CREATE TABLE

Let's explore how to set these constraints using the `CREATE TABLE` statement. We'll use a hypothetical "Products" table as an example:

sql

```sql
CREATE TABLE Products (
    ProductID INT PRIMARY KEY,
    ProductName VARCHAR(255) NOT NULL,
    Price DECIMAL(10, 2) DEFAULT 0.00,
    StockQuantity INT CHECK (StockQuantity >= 0),
    Barcode UNIQUE
);
```

In this example:

- `ProductID` is the primary key, ensuring that each product has a unique identifier.

- `ProductName` cannot be NULL, meaning every product must have a name.

- `Price` has a default value of 0.00, so if no price is specified during insertion, it defaults to zero.

- `StockQuantity` is constrained by a CHECK constraint, ensuring that it's always non-negative.

- `Barcode` must be unique for each product, preventing duplicate barcodes.

PRIMARY KEY Constraint

The PRIMARY KEY constraint is used to uniquely identify each row in a table. It ensures that the values in the specified column(s) are unique and not NULL. A table can have only one primary key.

Example: Creating a Table with a Primary Key

sql

```
CREATE TABLE Students (
    StudentID INT PRIMARY KEY,
    FirstName VARCHAR(50),
    LastName VARCHAR(50)
);
```

In this "Students" table, the `StudentID` column is designated as the primary key, ensuring that each student is uniquely identified by their ID.

UNIQUE Constraint

The UNIQUE constraint enforces that all values in a column are unique across rows in the table. Unlike the primary key, multiple columns can have unique constraints.

Example: Creating a Table with Unique Constraint

sql

```
CREATE TABLE Employees (
    EmployeeID INT PRIMARY KEY,
    SSN VARCHAR(9) UNIQUE,
    Email VARCHAR(100) UNIQUE
);
```

In this "Employees" table, both the `SSN` (Social Security Number) and `Email` columns have unique constraints, ensuring that no two employees can share the same SSN or email address.

NOT NULL Constraint

The NOT NULL constraint ensures that a column must always contain a value and cannot be left empty (NULL). This is commonly used for columns that must have data.

Example: Creating a Table with NOT NULL Constraint

sql

```
CREATE TABLE Customers (
    CustomerID INT PRIMARY KEY,
    FirstName VARCHAR(50) NOT NULL,
    LastName VARCHAR(50) NOT NULL,
    Email VARCHAR(100)
);
```

In this "Customers" table, both the `FirstName` and `LastName` columns are marked as NOT NULL, ensuring that every customer record must have values for these columns. The `Email` column, on the other hand, can be NULL.

DEFAULT Constraint

The DEFAULT constraint specifies a default value for a column when no value is provided during insertion. It is useful for providing default values or placeholders.

Example: Creating a Table with DEFAULT Constraint

sql

```
CREATE TABLE Orders (
    OrderID INT PRIMARY KEY,
    OrderDate DATE DEFAULT CURRENT_DATE,
    Status VARCHAR(20) DEFAULT 'Pending'
);
```

In this "Orders" table, the `OrderDate` column has a DEFAULT constraint set to `CURRENT_DATE`, which means if no order date is provided, it defaults to the current date. Similarly, the `Status` column has a DEFAULT constraint set to 'Pending'.

CHECK Constraint

The CHECK constraint defines a condition that values in a column must meet. If the condition is not met, the data insertion or update is rejected. CHECK constraints are used to enforce business rules or validate data.

Example: Creating a Table with CHECK Constraint

sql

```
CREATE TABLE Products (
    ProductID INT PRIMARY KEY,
    ProductName VARCHAR(255),
    Price DECIMAL(10, 2),
    StockQuantity INT CHECK (StockQuantity >= 0)
```

);

In this "Products" table, the CHECK constraint ensures that the `StockQuantity` column always contains non-negative values. If an attempt is made to insert a negative value, the constraint will prevent it.

Conclusion

Setting data constraints when creating tables with the `CREATE TABLE` statement is essential for maintaining data integrity and ensuring the accuracy of your database. By understanding and applying constraints such as PRIMARY KEY, UNIQUE, NOT NULL, DEFAULT, and CHECK, you can design tables that enforce rules, prevent data anomalies, and support the integrity of your data. Mastering these constraints is a key skill for anyone working with relational databases.

3.2 Modifying Table Structure with ALTER TABLE

3.2.1. Adding New Columns to a Table

In the realm of database management, tables are not static entities. Over time, your data requirements may change, and you might need to alter your existing tables to accommodate these changes. One common modification is adding new columns to a table. In this section, we will explore the `ALTER TABLE` statement and how to add new columns to an existing table.

Understanding ALTER TABLE

The `ALTER TABLE` statement in SQL allows you to make structural changes to an existing table, such as adding, modifying, or deleting columns. When you add new columns, you expand the capabilities of your table and enable it to store additional information without disrupting existing data.

Basic Syntax of ALTER TABLE for Adding Columns

The basic syntax for adding a new column to an existing table is as follows:

```sql
ALTER TABLE table_name
ADD column_name data_type;
```

Let's break down the components of this syntax:

- `table_name`: The name of the table to which you want to add a new column.

- `column_name`: The name of the new column you want to add.

- `data_type`: The data type of the new column, specifying the kind of data it will store.

Example: Adding a New Column

Let's say you have an existing "Customers" table with the following structure:

sql

```sql
CREATE TABLE Customers (
    CustomerID INT PRIMARY KEY,
    FirstName VARCHAR(50),
    LastName VARCHAR(50),
    Email VARCHAR(100)
);
```

Now, you want to add a new column called "Phone" to store customer phone numbers, which are of type VARCHAR:

sql

```sql
ALTER TABLE Customers
ADD Phone VARCHAR(15);
```

After executing this SQL statement, your "Customers" table will have a new "Phone" column:

sql

```
CREATE TABLE Customers (
    CustomerID INT PRIMARY KEY,
    FirstName VARCHAR(50),
    LastName VARCHAR(50),
    Email VARCHAR(100),
    Phone VARCHAR(15)
);
```

Adding Constraints to New Columns

When you add a new column, you can also specify constraints such as PRIMARY KEY, UNIQUE, NOT NULL, DEFAULT, or CHECK, just like you would when creating a new table.

Example: Adding a New Column with a Constraint

Let's add a "MembershipStatus" column to the "Customers" table, which will store the membership status of each customer. We want this column to have a default value of 'Regular':

sql

```
ALTER TABLE Customers
ADD MembershipStatus VARCHAR(20) DEFAULT 'Regular';
```

In this example, we've added a new column with a default constraint, ensuring that if no membership status is specified during insertion, it defaults to 'Regular'.

Adding a Column with Data

When you add a new column to an existing table, the new column initially contains NULL values for existing rows. Depending on your needs, you might want to populate this column with data for existing rows. You can achieve this using an `UPDATE` statement.

Example: Populating a New Column with Data

Suppose you've added a new column called "Country" to the "Customers" table, and you want to set the country for each customer:

sql

```sql
-- Add the new column with a default value
ALTER TABLE Customers
ADD Country VARCHAR(50) DEFAULT 'Unknown';


-- Update the new column with data
UPDATE Customers
SET Country = 'USA'
WHERE CustomerID = 1;
```

```
UPDATE Customers

SET Country = 'Canada'

WHERE CustomerID = 2;
```

```
-- Continue updating for other customers
```

In this example, we first add the "Country" column with a default value of 'Unknown'. Then, we use `UPDATE` statements to set the country for specific customers. You can repeat the `UPDATE` process for all customers as needed.

Considerations and Best Practices

When modifying table structures with `ALTER TABLE`, keep these considerations in mind:

1. Data Compatibility: Ensure that the data type you choose for the new column is compatible with the data it will store.

2. Data Migration: If you need to populate a new column with data for existing rows, plan and execute data migration strategies carefully.

3. Constraints: Think about whether the new column should have constraints, and if so, specify them during the column addition.

4. Testing: Before making structural changes to a production database, thoroughly test the changes in a development or staging environment.

Conclusion

The ability to modify table structures by adding new columns using the `ALTER TABLE` statement is a valuable skill for database administrators and developers. It allows you to adapt your database schema to evolving data requirements without the need to recreate the entire table. When adding new columns, you can also apply constraints to maintain data integrity and consistency. By following best practices and considering data compatibility, you can effectively manage and enhance your database schema as your application evolves.

3.2.2. Renaming Columns

In the ever-evolving landscape of database management, the need to update and refine table structures is commonplace. One such alteration is renaming columns within an existing table. In this section, we will delve into the `ALTER TABLE` statement and the process of renaming columns in a relational database.

Understanding ALTER TABLE

The `ALTER TABLE` statement in SQL is a versatile command used to make structural changes to existing tables. Among its capabilities is the ability to rename columns, which can be beneficial for various reasons, including improving clarity, consistency, or adherence to naming conventions.

Basic Syntax of ALTER TABLE for Renaming Columns

The fundamental syntax for renaming a column in an existing table is as follows:

sql

ALTER TABLE table_name

RENAME COLUMN old_column_name TO new_column_name;

Let's break down the components of this syntax:

- `table_name`: The name of the table containing the column you want to rename.

- `old_column_name`: The current name of the column you wish to change.

- `new_column_name`: The new name you want to assign to the column.

Example: Renaming a Column

Suppose you have a table called "Employees" with a column named "EmpName," and you want to rename it to "EmployeeName." Here's how you can achieve this using the `ALTER TABLE` statement:

sql

ALTER TABLE Employees

RENAME COLUMN EmpName TO EmployeeName;

After executing this SQL statement, the "Employees" table will reflect the updated column name:

sql

CREATE TABLE Employees (

　EmployeeID INT PRIMARY KEY,

    EmployeeName VARCHAR(50),

    LastName VARCHAR(50),

    Email VARCHAR(100)

);

Considerations for Renaming Columns

When renaming columns in an existing table, it's essential to consider the following factors:

1. Data Impact: Renaming a column does not affect the data stored within it. However, it changes the way you reference the column in future queries and applications.

2. Dependent Objects: Be aware of any dependent objects, such as views, stored procedures, or application code, that reference the column you're renaming. You may need to update these objects to reflect the new column name.

3. Schema Changes: Renaming columns is a structural change to the table. It's wise to perform such operations during scheduled maintenance or outside of peak usage times to minimize disruption.

4. Constraints and Indexes: If the column you're renaming is part of a constraint (e.g., a foreign key) or an index, ensure that the renaming process does not break these constraints. You may need to adjust them accordingly.

Renaming Columns with Constraints and Indexes

Renaming columns that are part of constraints or indexes requires special attention. You must ensure that these constraints and indexes remain valid after the renaming operation.

Example: Renaming a Column with a Constraint

Suppose you have a table "Orders" with a foreign key constraint on the "CustomerID" column, and you want to rename it to "ClientID." You need to consider the foreign key constraint and update it as well:

sql

```sql
-- First, drop the existing foreign key constraint
ALTER TABLE Orders
DROP CONSTRAINT fk_CustomerID;


-- Rename the column
ALTER TABLE Orders
RENAME COLUMN CustomerID TO ClientID;


-- Create a new foreign key constraint
ALTER TABLE Orders
ADD CONSTRAINT fk_ClientID
FOREIGN KEY (ClientID) REFERENCES Customers(CustomerID);
```

In this example, the foreign key constraint is dropped before renaming the column. After renaming, a new foreign key constraint is created with the updated column name.

Renaming Columns with Indexes

Renaming a column that is part of an index may also require updating the index to reflect the new column name:

sql

```
-- Rename the column
ALTER TABLE Employees
RENAME COLUMN EmpName TO EmployeeName;

-- Rename the index associated with the column
ALTER INDEX idx_EmpName RENAME TO idx_EmployeeName;
```

Here, we first rename the column "EmpName" to "EmployeeName" and then rename the associated index "idx_EmpName" to "idx_EmployeeName" to maintain consistency.

Conclusion

The ability to modify table structures, including renaming columns, using the `ALTER TABLE` statement is a valuable skill for database administrators and developers. Renaming columns can improve data clarity and consistency within a database, aligning it with naming conventions or evolving requirements. However, it's crucial to consider the impact on dependent objects, constraints, and indexes when renaming columns, and to perform such operations with caution to maintain data integrity. By mastering the art of column renaming, you can adapt your database schema to meet the changing needs of your application.

3.2.3. Removing Columns from a Table

In the realm of database management, maintaining a well-structured and efficient database schema is crucial. As data requirements evolve, you may find the need to make changes to your existing tables, including removing columns that are no longer needed. In this section, we will explore how to use the `ALTER TABLE` statement to remove columns from a table.

Understanding ALTER TABLE

The `ALTER TABLE` statement in SQL is a versatile command that allows you to make structural changes to existing database tables. One of the operations it supports is the removal of columns. Removing columns can help streamline your database schema, improve query performance, and reduce storage overhead.

Basic Syntax of ALTER TABLE for Removing Columns

The basic syntax for removing a column from an existing table is as follows:

sql

ALTER TABLE table_name

DROP COLUMN column_name;

Let's break down the components of this syntax:

- `table_name`: The name of the table from which you want to remove a column.

- `column_name`: The name of the column you want to drop.

Example: Removing a Column

Suppose you have a table called "Employees" with a column named "SocialSecurityNumber," and you want to remove this column from the table. Here's how you can achieve this using the `ALTER TABLE` statement:

sql

```sql
ALTER TABLE Employees

DROP COLUMN SocialSecurityNumber;
```

After executing this SQL statement, the "Employees" table will no longer contain the "SocialSecurityNumber" column:

sql

```sql
CREATE TABLE Employees (

    EmployeeID INT PRIMARY KEY,

    FirstName VARCHAR(50),

    LastName VARCHAR(50),

    Email VARCHAR(100)
);
```

Considerations for Removing Columns

When removing columns from an existing table, it's essential to consider the following factors:

1. Data Loss: Removing a column permanently deletes the data stored in that column for all rows in the table. Ensure that you have a backup or data migration plan in case the data is needed in the future.

2. Dependent Objects: Be aware of any dependent objects, such as views, stored procedures, or application code, that reference the column you're removing. You may need to update these objects to avoid errors.

3. Schema Cleanup: Removing columns can help declutter your schema and improve database performance, but it should be done judiciously. Consider whether the column is genuinely obsolete before removal.

4. Foreign Key Constraints: If the column you're removing is part of a foreign key constraint, you must also remove the constraint. This may involve altering other tables that reference the column.

Removing Columns with Foreign Key Constraints

When removing a column that is part of a foreign key constraint, you must take additional steps to maintain data integrity. First, you need to drop the foreign key constraint, then remove the column.

Example: Removing a Column with a Foreign Key Constraint

Suppose you have two tables, "Orders" and "Customers," where the "CustomerID" column in the "Orders" table references the "CustomerID" column in the "Customers" table. To remove the "CustomerID" column from the "Orders" table, follow these steps:

sql

-- Drop the foreign key constraint first

ALTER TABLE Orders

DROP CONSTRAINT fk_CustomerID;

-- Remove the column

ALTER TABLE Orders

DROP COLUMN CustomerID;

In this example, we first drop the foreign key constraint "fk_CustomerID" to avoid conflicts when removing the "CustomerID" column from the "Orders" table.

Removing Multiple Columns

You can remove multiple columns from a table in a single `ALTER TABLE` statement by specifying multiple `DROP COLUMN` clauses.

Example: Removing Multiple Columns

Suppose you have a table called "Inventory" with columns "ProductID," "ProductName," and "ProductDescription," and you want to remove both the "ProductName" and "ProductDescription" columns:

sql

ALTER TABLE Inventory

DROP COLUMN ProductName,

DROP COLUMN ProductDescription;

This single `ALTER TABLE` statement removes both columns from the "Inventory" table.

Conclusion

The ability to modify table structures, including removing columns using the `ALTER TABLE` statement, is a valuable skill for database administrators and developers. It allows you to adapt your database schema to changing data requirements and improve the efficiency of your database. However, it's crucial to consider data loss, dependent objects, foreign key constraints, and the necessity of column removal when making structural changes. By mastering the process of removing columns, you can maintain a well-organized and optimized database schema.

3.3 Deleting Tables with DROP TABLE

In the realm of database management, maintaining a streamlined and efficient database schema is essential. As data requirements change over time, you may find the need to remove entire tables that are no longer relevant or needed. In this section, we will explore how to use the `DROP TABLE` statement to delete tables in a relational database.

Understanding DROP TABLE

The `DROP TABLE` statement in SQL is a powerful command that allows you to permanently delete a table and all of its associated data and structures from the database. This operation is irreversible and should be used with caution, typically after careful consideration and data backup.

Basic Syntax of DROP TABLE

The basic syntax for deleting a table is straightforward:

```sql
DROP TABLE table_name;
```

Let's break down the components of this syntax:

- `table_name`: The name of the table you want to delete.

Example: Deleting a Table

Suppose you have a table called "ObsoleteData" that is no longer needed, and you want to delete it from the database. Here's how you can achieve this using the `DROP TABLE` statement:

sql

DROP TABLE ObsoleteData;

After executing this SQL statement, the "ObsoleteData" table, along with all its data and associated structures, is permanently removed from the database.

Considerations for Deleting Tables

Deleting tables using the `DROP TABLE` statement is a significant operation, and you should carefully consider the following factors:

1. Data Loss: Deleting a table results in the permanent loss of all data stored in that table. Ensure that you have backups or data migration plans in place to preserve important information if needed.

2. Foreign Key Constraints: If the table you're deleting is referenced by foreign key constraints in other tables, you must either drop those constraints or adjust them to avoid referential integrity issues.

3. Dependent Objects: Be aware of any dependent objects, such as views, stored procedures, or application code, that reference the table you're deleting. You may need to update or remove these objects to avoid errors.

4. Permissions: Ensure that you have the necessary permissions to delete a table. Database administrators typically have the authority to perform this operation.

Deleting Tables with Dependencies

When deleting a table that has dependencies, you must handle those dependencies appropriately to avoid errors and maintain data integrity. Here are steps you might follow when dealing with dependent objects:

1. Drop Dependent Foreign Key Constraints: If other tables have foreign key constraints that reference the table you're deleting, drop those constraints first. For example:

sql

```
ALTER TABLE Orders

DROP CONSTRAINT fk_CustomerID;
```

2. Drop Dependent Objects: Remove any dependent views, stored procedures, or triggers that reference the table:

sql

```
DROP VIEW my_view;

DROP PROCEDURE my_procedure;
```

3. Delete the Table: Finally, use the `DROP TABLE` statement to delete the table:

sql

DROP TABLE Customers;

Deleting Multiple Tables

You can delete multiple tables in a single SQL script by chaining `DROP TABLE` statements for each table you want to delete.

Example: Deleting Multiple Tables

Suppose you want to delete two tables, "Table1" and "Table2." You can do so in a single script like this:

sql

DROP TABLE Table1;

DROP TABLE Table2;

This script will delete both "Table1" and "Table2" and all their associated data.

Conclusion

The `DROP TABLE` statement is a powerful tool for database administrators and developers to maintain a well-structured and efficient database schema. When used judiciously, it allows you to remove tables that are no longer needed, streamlining your database and improving performance. However, the irreversible nature of table deletion means it should be approached with caution, considering data loss, dependencies, and permissions. By mastering the art of table deletion, you can keep your database schema clean and optimized for your evolving data needs.

PART IV
Filtering and Joining Tables

4.1 Combining Tables with JOIN

4.1.1. INNER JOIN

In the world of relational databases, the ability to combine data from multiple tables is fundamental. SQL provides powerful tools for this purpose, including the `JOIN` operation. In this section, we will explore the `INNER JOIN`, a commonly used type of join that allows you to retrieve data from two or more related tables based on a shared column.

Understanding the INNER JOIN

An `INNER JOIN` is a method of combining rows from two or more tables based on a related column between them. It retrieves only the rows that have matching values in both tables. This type of join is essential for querying data from multiple tables with relationships, such as primary keys and foreign keys.

Basic Syntax of INNER JOIN

The basic syntax of an `INNER JOIN` statement is as follows:

sql

SELECT columns

FROM table1

INNER JOIN table2

ON table1.column = table2.column;

Let's break down the components of this syntax:

- `columns`: The columns you want to retrieve from the joined tables.

- `table1` and `table2`: The names of the tables you want to join.

- `table1.column` and `table2.column`: The columns in the respective tables on which you want to join the data.

Example: Using INNER JOIN

Suppose you have two tables, "Orders" and "Customers," and you want to retrieve a list of orders along with the customer information for each order. You can achieve this by using an `INNER JOIN` on the "CustomerID" column, which is a common key between the two tables:

```sql
SELECT Orders.OrderID, Customers.CustomerName, Orders.OrderDate

FROM Orders

INNER JOIN Customers

ON Orders.CustomerID = Customers.CustomerID;
```

In this example, we are selecting columns from both the "Orders" and "Customers" tables and combining them using an `INNER JOIN`. The `ON` clause specifies the condition for the join, which is that the "CustomerID" in the "Orders" table must match the "CustomerID" in the "Customers" table.

Considerations for Using INNER JOIN

When using the `INNER JOIN` operation, there are several important considerations to keep in mind:

1. Common Column: Ensure that the columns you use for the join have matching values in both tables. In our example, the "CustomerID" column serves as the common link between "Orders" and "Customers."

2. Table Aliases: For tables with long names or when joining the same table multiple times, consider using table aliases to make your SQL queries more readable.

```sql
SELECT o.OrderID, c.CustomerName, o.OrderDate

FROM Orders AS o

INNER JOIN Customers AS c

ON o.CustomerID = c.CustomerID;
```

3. Column Ambiguity: If the joined tables have columns with the same name, you must qualify column names with table aliases to avoid ambiguity.

```sql
SELECT Orders.OrderID, Customers.CustomerName, Orders.OrderDate
```

FROM Orders

INNER JOIN Customers

ON Orders.CustomerID = Customers.CustomerID;

4. Filtering: You can further refine your results by adding a `WHERE` clause to the query. This allows you to filter the rows based on specific conditions.

sql

SELECT Orders.OrderID, Customers.CustomerName, Orders.OrderDate

FROM Orders

INNER JOIN Customers

ON Orders.CustomerID = Customers.CustomerID

WHERE Orders.OrderDate >= '2023-01-01';

Types of JOINs

In addition to the `INNER JOIN`, SQL offers other types of joins, including:

- **LEFT JOIN:** Retrieves all rows from the left table and the matching rows from the right table. If there is no match, NULL values are returned for columns from the right table.

- **RIGHT JOIN:** Retrieves all rows from the right table and the matching rows from the left table. If there is no match, NULL values are returned for columns from the left table.

- **FULL OUTER JOIN:** Retrieves all rows when there is a match in either the left or right table. NULL values are returned for columns where there is no match.

- SELF JOIN: Joins a table with itself to combine rows based on a related column within the same table.

Example: Using LEFT JOIN

Suppose you want to retrieve a list of all customers and their respective orders, including customers who haven't placed any orders. You can use a `LEFT JOIN` for this purpose:

sql

SELECT Customers.CustomerName, Orders.OrderID

FROM Customers

LEFT JOIN Orders

ON Customers.CustomerID = Orders.CustomerID;

In this example, the `LEFT JOIN` ensures that all customers are included in the result, regardless of whether they have placed orders.

Conclusion

The `INNER JOIN` is a powerful SQL operation for combining data from multiple tables based on shared columns. It is essential for retrieving related information efficiently and accurately in relational databases. By mastering the use of `INNER JOIN`, you can leverage the full potential of SQL to query and analyze data stored in complex, multi-table database schemas.

4.1.2. LEFT JOIN

In the realm of relational databases, joining tables is a fundamental operation when it comes to retrieving and analyzing data. SQL provides several types of joins, and in this section, we will delve into the world of `LEFT JOIN`. This type of join is invaluable when you want to retrieve data from one table along with related data from another table, while also including records that have no matches in the second table.

Understanding the LEFT JOIN

A `LEFT JOIN` is a type of join operation that combines rows from two or more tables based on a related column and includes all the rows from the left table (or the first table mentioned in the SQL statement) even if they don't have matching values in the right table. When there is no match in the right table, NULL values are returned for the columns from the right table.

Basic Syntax of LEFT JOIN

The basic syntax for a `LEFT JOIN` statement is as follows:

```sql
SELECT columns
FROM table1
LEFT JOIN table2
ON table1.column = table2.column;
```

Let's break down the components of this syntax:

- `columns`: The columns you want to retrieve from the joined tables.

- `table1` and `table2`: The names of the tables you want to join.

- `table1.column` and `table2.column`: The columns in the respective tables on which you want to join the data.

Example: Using LEFT JOIN

Suppose you have two tables, "Students" and "Grades," and you want to retrieve a list of all students along with their corresponding grade information, including students who haven't received any grades yet. You can achieve this by using a `LEFT JOIN` on the "StudentID" column, which is common between the two tables:

sql

SELECT Students.StudentID, Students.StudentName, Grades.Grade

FROM Students

LEFT JOIN Grades

ON Students.StudentID = Grades.StudentID;

In this example, we're selecting columns from both the "Students" and "Grades" tables and combining them using a `LEFT JOIN`. The `ON` clause specifies the condition for the join, which is that the "StudentID" in the "Students" table must match the "StudentID" in the "Grades" table.

Considerations for Using LEFT JOIN

When working with a `LEFT JOIN`, there are several important considerations to keep in mind:

1. Retrieving All Rows: A `LEFT JOIN` ensures that all rows from the left table are included in the result, even if they have no matching rows in the right table. This is particularly useful when you want to retrieve data from the left table and include associated data from the right table when available.

2. Handling NULL Values: When there is no match in the right table for a particular row in the left table, NULL values are returned for the columns from the right table. Be prepared to handle these NULL values in your query or application logic.

3. Column Aliases: Consider using column aliases for columns that have the same name in both tables to avoid ambiguity in your query results.

```sql
SELECT Students.StudentID, Students.StudentName, Grades.Grade AS StudentGrade
FROM Students
LEFT JOIN Grades
ON Students.StudentID = Grades.StudentID;
```

4. Filtering: You can further refine your results by adding a `WHERE` clause to the query. This allows you to filter the rows based on specific conditions.

```sql
SELECT Students.StudentID, Students.StudentName, Grades.Grade
FROM Students
LEFT JOIN Grades
ON Students.StudentID = Grades.StudentID
```

WHERE Grades.Grade >= 90;

When to Use LEFT JOIN

You should consider using a `LEFT JOIN` in the following scenarios:

- Retrieving data from one table along with related data from another table, ensuring that all rows from the first table are included.

- Analyzing data where you want to identify records with missing or incomplete related data.

Conclusion

The `LEFT JOIN` is a powerful SQL operation for combining data from multiple tables while preserving all rows from the left table, even when there are no matching rows in the right table. This makes it an invaluable tool for querying and analyzing data in relational databases. By mastering the use of `LEFT JOIN`, you can efficiently retrieve and work with data that spans multiple tables, gaining deeper insights into your database.

4.1.3. RIGHT JOIN

In the world of relational databases, joining tables is a crucial operation for retrieving and analyzing data from multiple sources. SQL provides various types of joins, and in this section, we will explore the `RIGHT JOIN`. This join is the counterpart of the `LEFT JOIN` and is used to retrieve all rows from the right table (or the second table mentioned in the SQL statement), along with matching rows from the left table.

Understanding the RIGHT JOIN

A `RIGHT JOIN`, also known as a `RIGHT OUTER JOIN`, combines rows from two or more tables based on a related column and includes all the rows from the right table (the second table mentioned) even if they don't have matching values in the left table. When there is no match in the left table, NULL values are returned for the columns from the left table.

Basic Syntax of RIGHT JOIN

The basic syntax for a `RIGHT JOIN` statement is as follows:

```sql
SELECT columns
FROM table1
RIGHT JOIN table2
ON table1.column = table2.column;
```

Let's break down the components of this syntax:

- `columns`: The columns you want to retrieve from the joined tables.

- `table1` and `table2`: The names of the tables you want to join.

- `table1.column` and `table2.column`: The columns in the respective tables on which you want to join the data.

Example: Using RIGHT JOIN

Suppose you have two tables, "Orders" and "Customers," and you want to retrieve a list of all customers along with their corresponding order information, including orders from customers who haven't placed any orders yet. You can achieve this by using a `RIGHT JOIN` on the "CustomerID" column, which is common between the two tables:

sql

```
SELECT Customers.CustomerID, Customers.CustomerName, Orders.OrderDate
FROM Customers
RIGHT JOIN Orders
ON Customers.CustomerID = Orders.CustomerID;
```

In this example, we're selecting columns from both the "Customers" and "Orders" tables and combining them using a `RIGHT JOIN`. The `ON` clause specifies the condition for the join, which is that the "CustomerID" in the "Customers" table must match the "CustomerID" in the "Orders" table.

Considerations for Using RIGHT JOIN

When working with a `RIGHT JOIN`, there are several important considerations to keep in mind:

1. Retrieving All Rows from the Right Table: A `RIGHT JOIN` ensures that all rows from the right table are included in the result, even if they have no matching rows in the left table. This is particularly useful when you want to retrieve data from the right table and include associated data from the left table when available.

2. Handling NULL Values: When there is no match in the left table for a particular row in the right table, NULL values are returned for the columns from the left table. Be prepared to handle these NULL values in your query or application logic.

3. Column Aliases: Consider using column aliases for columns that have the same name in both tables to avoid ambiguity in your query results.

sql

```
SELECT Customers.CustomerID, Customers.CustomerName, Orders.OrderDate AS OrderDate
FROM Customers
RIGHT JOIN Orders
ON Customers.CustomerID = Orders.CustomerID;
```

4. Filtering: You can further refine your results by adding a `WHERE` clause to the query. This allows you to filter the rows based on specific conditions.

sql

```
SELECT Customers.CustomerID, Customers.CustomerName, Orders.OrderDate
FROM Customers
RIGHT JOIN Orders
ON Customers.CustomerID = Orders.CustomerID
WHERE Orders.OrderDate >= '2023-01-01';
```

When to Use RIGHT JOIN

You should consider using a `RIGHT JOIN` in the following scenarios:

- Retrieving data from one table along with related data from another table, ensuring that all rows from the second table are included.

- Analyzing data where you want to identify records with missing or incomplete related data.

Conclusion

The `RIGHT JOIN` is a valuable SQL operation for combining data from multiple tables while ensuring that all rows from the right table are included in the result, even when there are no matching rows in the left table. This makes it an essential tool for querying and analyzing data in relational databases. By mastering the use of `RIGHT JOIN`, you can efficiently retrieve and work with data that spans multiple tables, gaining deeper insights into your database.

4.1.4. FULL OUTER JOIN

In the realm of relational databases, combining data from multiple tables is a common and essential task. SQL provides several types of join operations, and in this section, we will explore the versatile `FULL OUTER JOIN`. This join retrieves all rows from both the left and right tables and includes matching rows as well as unmatched rows, providing a comprehensive view of the data.

Understanding the FULL OUTER JOIN

A `FULL OUTER JOIN`, also known as a `FULL JOIN`, combines rows from two or more tables based on a related column and includes all rows from both tables, regardless of whether they have matching values in the other table. When there is no match in one of the tables, NULL values are returned for the columns from that table.

Basic Syntax of FULL OUTER JOIN

The basic syntax for a `FULL OUTER JOIN` statement is as follows:

```sql
SELECT columns
FROM table1
FULL OUTER JOIN table2
ON table1.column = table2.column;
```

Let's break down the components of this syntax:

- `columns`: The columns you want to retrieve from the joined tables.

- `table1` and `table2`: The names of the tables you want to join.

- `table1.column` and `table2.column`: The columns in the respective tables on which you want to join the data.

Example: Using FULL OUTER JOIN

Suppose you have two tables, "Employees" and "Departments," and you want to retrieve a list of all employees along with their corresponding department information. You also want to include departments that have no employees and employees who have not been assigned to a department. You can achieve this by using a `FULL OUTER JOIN` on the "DepartmentID" column, which is common between the two tables:

```sql
SELECT Employees.EmployeeID, Employees.EmployeeName, Departments.DepartmentName
```

```sql
FROM Employees

FULL OUTER JOIN Departments

ON Employees.DepartmentID = Departments.DepartmentID;
```

In this example, we're selecting columns from both the "Employees" and "Departments" tables and combining them using a `FULL OUTER JOIN`. The `ON` clause specifies the condition for the join, which is that the "DepartmentID" in the "Employees" table must match the "DepartmentID" in the "Departments" table.

Considerations for Using FULL OUTER JOIN

When working with a `FULL OUTER JOIN`, there are several important considerations to keep in mind:

1. Retrieving All Rows: A `FULL OUTER JOIN` ensures that all rows from both the left and right tables are included in the result, making it suitable for scenarios where you want a comprehensive view of the data.

2. Handling NULL Values: When there is no match in one of the tables for a particular row, NULL values are returned for the columns from that table. Be prepared to handle these NULL values in your query or application logic.

3. Column Aliases: Consider using column aliases for columns that have the same name in both tables to avoid ambiguity in your query results.

sql

```sql
SELECT Employees.EmployeeID, Employees.EmployeeName,
Departments.DepartmentName AS EmployeeDepartment

FROM Employees

FULL OUTER JOIN Departments

ON Employees.DepartmentID = Departments.DepartmentID;
```

4. Filtering: You can further refine your results by adding a `WHERE` clause to the query. This allows you to filter the rows based on specific conditions.

```sql
sql

SELECT Employees.EmployeeID, Employees.EmployeeName,
Departments.DepartmentName

FROM Employees

FULL OUTER JOIN Departments

ON Employees.DepartmentID = Departments.DepartmentID

WHERE Employees.EmployeeSalary >= 50000;
```

When to Use FULL OUTER JOIN

You should consider using a `FULL OUTER JOIN` in the following scenarios:

- Retrieving a comprehensive view of data from two tables, including all rows from both tables.

- Analyzing data where you want to identify records with missing or incomplete related data in either table.

Conclusion

The `FULL OUTER JOIN` is a versatile SQL operation for combining data from multiple tables while ensuring that all rows from both tables are included in the result, regardless of matching values. This join provides a comprehensive view of the data, making it an invaluable tool for querying and analyzing data in relational databases. By mastering the use of `FULL OUTER JOIN`, you can efficiently retrieve and work with data that spans multiple tables, gaining a complete understanding of your database.

4.2 Combining Tables with JOIN

In the world of SQL, the ability to filter and narrow down your results is crucial for obtaining the specific data you need from joined tables. When combining tables using joins, it's common to want to further refine the results to meet your criteria. This is where the `WHERE` clause comes into play, allowing you to filter data in joined results effectively.

Understanding the WHERE Clause in Joined Queries

The `WHERE` clause in SQL is used to filter rows from the result set based on specified conditions. When used in conjunction with joins, it allows you to apply conditions not only to individual tables but also to the joined results. This means you can filter data based on columns from any of the tables involved in the join.

Basic Syntax of WHERE Clause in Joined Queries

The basic syntax of using the `WHERE` clause in a joined query is as follows:

```sql
SELECT columns
FROM table1
INNER JOIN table2 ON table1.column = table2.column
WHERE condition;
```

Here's a breakdown of the components:

- `columns`: The columns you want to retrieve from the joined tables.

- `table1` and `table2`: The names of the tables you're joining.

- `table1.column` and `table2.column`: The columns in the respective tables that you're using to establish the join relationship.

- `condition`: The condition you want to apply to filter the joined results.

Example: Filtering Joined Data

Suppose you have two tables, "Orders" and "Customers," and you want to retrieve a list of orders along with customer information for orders placed after January 1, 2023. You can achieve this by using an `INNER JOIN` to combine the tables on the "CustomerID" column and then applying a `WHERE` clause to filter based on the "OrderDate" column:

sql

SELECT Orders.OrderID, Customers.CustomerName, Orders.OrderDate

FROM Orders

INNER JOIN Customers ON Orders.CustomerID = Customers.CustomerID

WHERE Orders.OrderDate >= '2023-01-01';

In this example, we're selecting columns from both the "Orders" and "Customers" tables using an `INNER JOIN`. The `ON` clause specifies the condition for the join, which is the matching "CustomerID" values in both tables. We then use the `WHERE` clause to filter the results based on the "OrderDate."

Considerations for Using WHERE in Joined Queries

When filtering data in joined results using the `WHERE` clause, keep the following considerations in mind:

1. Column Qualification: To avoid ambiguity, it's a good practice to qualify column names with table aliases. This helps SQL identify which table a column belongs to, especially when multiple tables have columns with the same name.

```sql
SELECT O.OrderID, C.CustomerName, O.OrderDate

FROM Orders AS O

INNER JOIN Customers AS C ON O.CustomerID = C.CustomerID

WHERE O.OrderDate >= '2023-01-01';
```

2. Filtering on Any Column: You can filter on any column from the joined tables, not just the columns used in the join condition. This gives you flexibility in crafting your filtering criteria.

3. Multiple Conditions: You can use multiple conditions in the `WHERE` clause by combining them using logical operators such as `AND` and `OR`. This allows for complex filtering logic.

```sql
SELECT ...

FROM table1

INNER JOIN table2 ON ...

WHERE condition1 AND condition2;
```

4. Filtering Outer Joins: When using outer joins (e.g., `LEFT JOIN`, `RIGHT JOIN`, or `FULL OUTER JOIN`), be aware that filtering in the `WHERE` clause can affect the result set differently than when using inner joins. Rows with NULL values may be included or excluded based on your conditions.

Conclusion

The `WHERE` clause in joined queries is a powerful tool for refining your results and extracting the specific data you need from combined tables. Whether you're working with inner joins or outer joins, the `WHERE` clause allows you to apply filtering conditions to create tailored result sets. By understanding how to use the `WHERE` clause effectively in joined queries, you can extract valuable insights from your database and make informed decisions based on your filtered data.

4.3 Combining Multiple Tables

In the world of relational databases, scenarios often arise where you need to combine data from more than two tables to retrieve meaningful and comprehensive information. SQL provides mechanisms for handling such situations by joining multiple tables in a single query. In this section, we'll explore the techniques for combining multiple tables effectively.

Understanding Joining Multiple Tables

When you need to work with data stored across multiple tables, you can use SQL joins to connect these tables together. SQL supports joining any number of tables in a query, and the process involves linking each table to the next using appropriate join conditions.

Basic Syntax for Joining Multiple Tables

The basic syntax for joining multiple tables in SQL involves extending the previous join statements for each additional table. Here's a general template:

```sql
SELECT columns
FROM table1
JOIN table2 ON table1.column = table2.column
JOIN table3 ON table2.column = table3.column
-- Add more JOIN clauses as needed
WHERE condition;
```

Let's break down the components:

- `columns`: The columns you want to retrieve from the joined tables.

- `table1`, `table2`, `table3`, etc.: The names of the tables you want to join.

- `table1.column`, `table2.column`, `table3.column`, etc.: The columns in the respective tables that you're using to establish join relationships.

- `condition`: The condition you want to apply to filter the results.

Example: Joining Multiple Tables

Suppose you have three tables: "Orders," "Customers," and "Products." You want to retrieve a list of orders along with customer and product information for orders placed after January 1, 2023. To achieve this, you can use multiple joins:

sql

```sql
SELECT    Orders.OrderID,    Customers.CustomerName,    Products.ProductName,
Orders.OrderDate

FROM Orders

JOIN Customers ON Orders.CustomerID = Customers.CustomerID

JOIN Products ON Orders.ProductID = Products.ProductID

WHERE Orders.OrderDate >= '2023-01-01';
```

In this example, we're performing two joins—one to link "Orders" with "Customers" based on the "CustomerID" column and another to link "Orders" with "Products" based on the "ProductID" column. The `WHERE` clause is used to filter the results based on the "OrderDate."

Considerations for Joining Multiple Tables

When combining multiple tables in SQL, keep the following considerations in mind:

1. Join Order: The order in which you specify the tables and join conditions can affect the query's performance and results. It's generally a good practice to put more selective tables (those that reduce the result set size) earlier in the join sequence.

2. Table Aliases: As you work with more tables, table aliases become increasingly important to avoid naming conflicts and improve query readability. Assign meaningful aliases to tables to make your code more self-explanatory.

```sql
SELECT O.OrderID, C.CustomerName, P.ProductName, O.OrderDate

FROM Orders AS O

JOIN Customers AS C ON O.CustomerID = C.CustomerID

JOIN Products AS P ON O.ProductID = P.ProductID

WHERE O.OrderDate >= '2023-01-01';
```

3. Filtering: Be cautious when applying filtering conditions. Ensure that the conditions you use in the `WHERE` clause are relevant to the specific data you want to retrieve, as they can significantly impact query results.

4. Performance: Joining multiple tables can be resource-intensive, especially with large datasets. Be mindful of query performance and consider using indexes on join columns for optimization.

Conclusion

Combining multiple tables in SQL queries allows you to extract comprehensive and meaningful insights from complex datasets. By joining tables effectively and using appropriate filtering conditions, you can retrieve precisely the data you need for analysis and reporting. Understanding the techniques for joining multiple tables empowers you to work with diverse data sources, enabling you to make data-driven decisions and gain deeper insights into your database.

PART V
Summarizing and Grouping Data

5.1 Calculating Summaries with Aggregate Functions

5.1.1. COUNT, SUM, AVG, MIN, MAX

In the world of SQL, it's often essential to summarize and aggregate data to gain meaningful insights and answer specific questions about your dataset. SQL provides a set of powerful aggregate functions that allow you to perform calculations on groups of rows. In this section, we'll explore the most commonly used aggregate functions: `COUNT`, `SUM`, `AVG`, `MIN`, and `MAX`.

Understanding Aggregate Functions

Aggregate functions operate on sets of rows and return a single result value for each group of rows. These functions are typically used with the `GROUP BY` clause to divide the dataset into groups based on one or more columns. Then, the aggregate function is applied to each group, producing a summary value.

Common Aggregate Functions

Let's dive into the details of each common aggregate function:

1. `COUNT` Function:

- **Purpose**: Counts the number of rows in a group.

- **Syntax:** `COUNT(expression)` or `COUNT(*)`

- **Example**: Count the number of orders for each customer.

```sql
SELECT CustomerID, COUNT(*) AS OrderCount
FROM Orders
GROUP BY CustomerID;
```

2. `SUM` Function:

- **Purpose**: Calculates the sum of values in a numeric column for a group.

- **Syntax**: `SUM(column)`

- **Example**: Calculate the total order amount for each customer.

```sql
SELECT CustomerID, SUM(OrderAmount) AS TotalAmount
FROM Orders
GROUP BY CustomerID;
```

3. `AVG` Function:

- **Purpose:** Calculates the average (mean) value of a numeric column for a group.

- **Syntax**: `AVG(column)`

- **Example**: Calculate the average order amount for each customer.

```sql
SELECT CustomerID, AVG(OrderAmount) AS AverageAmount
FROM Orders
GROUP BY CustomerID;
```

4. `MIN` Function:

- **Purpose**: Finds the minimum value in a column for a group.

- **Syntax**: `MIN(column)`

- **Example**: Find the smallest order amount for each customer.

```sql
SELECT CustomerID, MIN(OrderAmount) AS MinAmount
FROM Orders
GROUP BY CustomerID;
```

5. `MAX` Function:

- **Purpose**: Finds the maximum value in a column for a group.

- **Syntax:** `MAX(column)`

- **Example**: Find the largest order amount for each customer.

sql

SELECT CustomerID, MAX(OrderAmount) AS MaxAmount

FROM Orders

GROUP BY CustomerID;

Using Aggregate Functions with GROUP BY

To utilize aggregate functions effectively, you typically pair them with the `GROUP BY` clause. The `GROUP BY` clause divides the dataset into groups based on the specified column(s). Then, the aggregate function calculates the summary value for each group.

Example: Calculating Summaries

Suppose you have an "Orders" table with columns "CustomerID" and "OrderAmount," and you want to calculate the total order amount, average order amount, and the number of orders for each customer. Here's how you can achieve this using aggregate functions and `GROUP BY`:

sql

SELECT CustomerID, COUNT(*) AS OrderCount, SUM(OrderAmount) AS TotalAmount, AVG(OrderAmount) AS AverageAmount

FROM Orders

```
GROUP BY CustomerID;
```

In this example, we group the data by "CustomerID" and calculate the count, sum, and average of "OrderAmount" for each customer.

Conclusion

Aggregate functions are essential tools in SQL for summarizing and gaining insights from your data. Whether you need to count, sum, find averages, or determine minimum and maximum values, these functions provide valuable information about your dataset. When combined with the `GROUP BY` clause, you can segment your data into meaningful groups and perform calculations on each group, enabling you to make informed decisions and extract valuable statistics from your database.

5.1.2. GROUP BY

In the previous section, we discussed how aggregate functions like `COUNT`, `SUM`, `AVG`, `MIN`, and `MAX` can help you perform calculations on your dataset. While these functions are powerful on their own, they become even more valuable when combined with the `GROUP BY` clause. The `GROUP BY` clause allows you to group rows that share a common attribute, and then apply aggregate functions to those groups. This enables you to generate summary reports and gain deeper insights into your data.

Understanding the GROUP BY Clause

The `GROUP BY` clause is used to group rows from a table based on the values in one or more columns. When you use `GROUP BY`, the result set is divided into groups, with each group representing a unique combination of the grouped columns' values. Aggregate functions can then be applied to these groups to calculate summary values.

Syntax of the GROUP BY Clause:

sql

SELECT column1, column2, aggregate_function(column)

FROM table

GROUP BY column1, column2;

- `column1`, `column2`, ...: The columns by which you want to group the data.

- `aggregate_function(column)`: The aggregate function applied to each group.

Example: Grouping Data by Category

Let's say you have a "Products" table with columns "Category" and "Price," and you want to find the average price of products within each category. You can achieve this using the `GROUP BY` clause and the `AVG` aggregate function:

sql

SELECT Category, AVG(Price) AS AveragePrice

FROM Products

GROUP BY Category;

In this example, the data is grouped by the "Category" column, and the `AVG` function calculates the average price for each category. The result is a list of categories along with their respective average prices.

Using GROUP BY with Multiple Columns

You can also use `GROUP BY` with multiple columns to create more granular groups. For example, if you have a "Sales" table with columns "Region," "Month," and "SalesAmount," and you want to find the total sales amount for each region and month combination, you can use:

sql

SELECT Region, Month, SUM(SalesAmount) AS TotalSales

FROM Sales

GROUP BY Region, Month;

This query groups the data by both "Region" and "Month," allowing you to calculate total sales amounts for each region-month combination.

Filtering Groups with HAVING

In addition to the `GROUP BY` clause, you can use the `HAVING` clause to filter groups based on aggregate function results. This is especially useful when you want to include or exclude groups based on specific criteria.

Syntax of the HAVING Clause:

sql

SELECT column1, column2, aggregate_function(column)

FROM table

GROUP BY column1, column2

HAVING aggregate_function(column) condition;

- `condition`: The condition used to filter groups.

Example: Filtering Groups with HAVING

Suppose you have a "Customers" table with columns "CustomerID" and "TotalOrders," and you want to find customers who have placed more than five orders. You can use the `HAVING` clause with the `COUNT` function:

sql

SELECT CustomerID, COUNT(OrderID) AS TotalOrders

FROM Orders

GROUP BY CustomerID

HAVING COUNT(OrderID) > 5;

In this query, the `COUNT` function is used to calculate the total number of orders for each customer. The `HAVING` clause filters the results to include only customers with more than five orders.

Conclusion

The `GROUP BY` clause is a powerful tool in SQL that allows you to group rows based on common attributes and perform aggregate calculations on those groups. By using aggregate functions in combination with `GROUP BY`, you can generate summary reports, calculate statistics, and gain insights into your data. Additionally, the `HAVING` clause provides a way to filter groups based on aggregate results, further enhancing your ability to extract meaningful information from your database. Understanding how to use these clauses effectively is key to becoming proficient in SQL data analysis and reporting.

5.1.3. HAVING

In the world of SQL, the `HAVING` clause plays a critical role in data summarization and filtering. While the `WHERE` clause filters rows before they are grouped, the `HAVING` clause filters the grouped results after the `GROUP BY` operation, allowing you to apply conditions to groups based on aggregate values. This enables you to fine-tune your summary queries and extract specific subsets of data from your dataset.

Understanding the HAVING Clause

The `HAVING` clause is typically used with the `GROUP BY` clause to filter groups of rows based on the result of an aggregate function. It allows you to specify conditions that groups must meet in order to be included in the result set. In essence, `HAVING` lets you filter grouped data based on summary values, such as counts, sums, averages, minimums, or maximums.

Syntax of the HAVING Clause:

sql

SELECT column1, column2, aggregate_function(column)

FROM table

GROUP BY column1, column2

HAVING aggregate_function(column) condition;

- `column1`, `column2`, ...: The columns by which you want to group the data.

- `aggregate_function(column)`: The aggregate function applied to each group.

- `condition`: The condition used to filter groups.

Example: Filtering Groups with HAVING

Suppose you have a "Customers" table with columns "CustomerID" and "TotalOrders," and you want to find customers who have placed more than five orders. You can use the `HAVING` clause with the `COUNT` function:

sql

SELECT CustomerID, COUNT(OrderID) AS TotalOrders

FROM Orders

GROUP BY CustomerID

HAVING COUNT(OrderID) > 5;

In this query, the `COUNT` function calculates the total number of orders for each customer, and the `HAVING` clause filters the results to include only customers with more than five orders.

Combining HAVING with Other Conditions

One of the strengths of the `HAVING` clause is its ability to combine conditions with logical operators like `AND` and `OR`. This allows you to specify complex criteria for filtering groups based on aggregate values.

Example: Combining HAVING Conditions

Let's say you have a "Sales" table with columns "Region," "Month," and "SalesAmount," and you want to find regions where the total sales amount for January is greater than $10,000 or the total sales amount for February is greater than $15,000. You can use the `HAVING` clause with the `SUM` function and logical operators:

sql

```
SELECT Region, SUM(SalesAmount) AS TotalSales

FROM Sales

GROUP BY Region

HAVING SUM(CASE WHEN Month = 'January' THEN SalesAmount ELSE 0 END) > 10000

    OR SUM(CASE WHEN Month = 'February' THEN SalesAmount ELSE 0 END) > 15000;
```

In this query, we calculate the total sales amount for each region, but we filter the results using the `HAVING` clause to include only regions that meet the specified criteria for January or February.

Using HAVING with Different Aggregate Functions

You can also use the `HAVING` clause with different aggregate functions within the same query. This allows you to apply various summary conditions to your data.

Example: Using Multiple Aggregate Functions with HAVING

Suppose you have an "Employees" table with columns "Department" and "Salary," and you want to find departments where the average salary is greater than $60,000, and the total number of employees is more than five. You can use both `AVG` and `COUNT` functions in the `HAVING` clause:

sql

```
SELECT Department, AVG(Salary) AS AverageSalary, COUNT(EmployeeID) AS EmployeeCount

FROM Employees

GROUP BY Department

HAVING AVG(Salary) > 60000 AND COUNT(EmployeeID) > 5;
```

In this query, we calculate the average salary and count of employees for each department. The `HAVING` clause filters the results to include only departments that meet both conditions.

Conclusion

The `HAVING` clause is a crucial component of SQL when it comes to summarizing and filtering grouped data. It enables you to apply conditions to groups based on aggregate values, allowing you to extract specific subsets of data that meet your criteria. By combining `HAVING` with the `GROUP BY` clause and various aggregate functions, you can perform complex data summarization and analysis tasks, providing valuable insights into your dataset. Understanding how to use `HAVING` effectively is essential for anyone working with SQL and seeking to extract meaningful information from their data.

PART VI
Data Constraints and Indexing

6.1 Implementing Data Constraints

6.1.1. PRIMARY KEY Constraint

In the world of databases, ensuring data accuracy and integrity is of paramount importance. One of the key tools for achieving this is the use of data constraints. In SQL, the `PRIMARY KEY` constraint is a fundamental data constraint that plays a crucial role in maintaining the quality and consistency of your data.

Understanding the PRIMARY KEY Constraint

The `PRIMARY KEY` constraint is used to uniquely identify each record in a database table. It ensures that no two rows in the table have the same values in the specified column or columns. The primary key serves as a reference point for establishing relationships between tables, enforcing data integrity, and optimizing database performance.

Syntax of the PRIMARY KEY Constraint:

sql

CREATE TABLE table_name

(

  column1 data_type PRIMARY KEY,

  column2 data_type,

...

);

- `table_name`: The name of the table you're creating.

- `column1`, `column2`, ...: The columns that make up the primary key.

- `data_type`: The data type of each column.

Example: Creating a Table with a PRIMARY KEY

Let's say you want to create a "Students" table where each student is uniquely identified by their "StudentID." You can use the `PRIMARY KEY` constraint as follows:

```sql
CREATE TABLE Students
(
    StudentID INT PRIMARY KEY,
    FirstName VARCHAR(50),
    LastName VARCHAR(50),
    Age INT
);
```

In this example, the "StudentID" column is designated as the primary key, ensuring that each student has a unique identifier.

Benefits of the PRIMARY KEY Constraint

1. Uniqueness: The primary key constraint enforces the uniqueness of values in the designated column(s). This prevents duplicate records in the table, ensuring data accuracy.

2. Data Integrity: It helps maintain data integrity by preventing invalid or incomplete data from being entered into the table. Each record must have a unique identifier.

3. Relationships: Primary keys are used as references in establishing relationships between tables. For example, in a relational database, you might have a foreign key in another table that points to the primary key of this table.

4. Indexing: Primary keys are automatically indexed by most database management systems (DBMS). This means that data retrieval is optimized when searching for records based on the primary key.

Inserting Data with a PRIMARY KEY

When inserting data into a table with a primary key, you must ensure that the values in the primary key column(s) are unique. If you attempt to insert a record with a duplicate primary key value, the DBMS will raise an error, and the insertion will fail.

Example: Inserting Data with a PRIMARY KEY

Assuming you have the "Students" table with a primary key on "StudentID," here's how you can insert a new student record:

sql

```
INSERT INTO Students (StudentID, FirstName, LastName, Age)

VALUES (1, 'John', 'Doe', 20);
```

This insertion will succeed because the "StudentID" value (1) is unique. However, if you attempt to insert another record with the same "StudentID," it will result in an error.

Conclusion

The `PRIMARY KEY` constraint is a fundamental tool in SQL for maintaining data accuracy and integrity. It ensures that each record in a table is uniquely identified and plays a crucial role in establishing relationships between tables in a relational database. By enforcing uniqueness and optimizing data retrieval through indexing, the primary key constraint is an essential concept for anyone working with databases and SQL. Understanding how to implement and manage primary keys is key to building robust and efficient database systems.

6.1.2. FOREIGN KEY Constraint

In the realm of database management, maintaining the relationships between tables is essential for data accuracy and integrity. SQL provides the `FOREIGN KEY` constraint, a powerful tool that enforces referential integrity by establishing links between tables. This constraint ensures that data relationships are maintained and that data consistency is preserved.

Understanding the FOREIGN KEY Constraint

The `FOREIGN KEY` constraint is used to link two tables together based on a column or a set of columns. It creates a relationship between the referencing (child) table and the referenced (parent) table. This relationship is crucial for ensuring that the data in the child table aligns with the data in the parent table, preventing orphaned records and maintaining referential integrity.

Syntax of the FOREIGN KEY Constraint:

sql

```
CREATE TABLE table_name
(
  column1 data_type,
  column2 data_type,
  ...
  FOREIGN KEY (column1) REFERENCES parent_table(parent_column)
);
```

- `table_name`: The name of the table you're creating.

- `column1`, `column2`, ...: The columns in the child table.

- `data_type`: The data type of each column.

- `parent_table`: The name of the referenced parent table.

- `parent_column`: The column in the parent table that the child table's column references.

Example: Creating a Table with a FOREIGN KEY

Let's consider a scenario where you have two tables, "Orders" and "Customers." Each order in the "Orders" table should be associated with a customer in the "Customers" table. You can use the `FOREIGN KEY` constraint to create this relationship:

sql

```
CREATE TABLE Customers

(

    CustomerID INT PRIMARY KEY,

    FirstName VARCHAR(50),

    LastName VARCHAR(50)

);


CREATE TABLE Orders

(

    OrderID INT PRIMARY KEY,

    OrderDate DATE,

    CustomerID INT,

    FOREIGN KEY (CustomerID) REFERENCES Customers(CustomerID)

);
```

In this example, the "CustomerID" column in the "Orders" table is designated as a foreign key that references the "CustomerID" column in the "Customers" table. This relationship ensures that each order is associated with a valid customer, maintaining data consistency.

Actions Performed by the FOREIGN KEY Constraint

The `FOREIGN KEY` constraint performs several actions to maintain referential integrity:

1. Validation: When inserting or updating data in the child table, the `FOREIGN KEY` constraint verifies that the values in the foreign key column(s) exist in the parent table. If they don't, the constraint prevents the operation, maintaining data accuracy.

2. Cascade Updates: You can specify what happens when a referenced row in the parent table is updated. Common options include cascading the update to the child rows or setting the foreign key values to NULL.

3. Cascade Deletes: Similarly, you can define the behavior when a referenced row in the parent table is deleted. You can choose to cascade the delete operation to the child rows, restrict the deletion if child rows exist, or set foreign key values to NULL.

Inserting Data with FOREIGN KEY Constraints

When inserting data into a table with a foreign key constraint, you must ensure that the values in the foreign key column(s) correspond to existing values in the referenced table. Otherwise, the DBMS will raise an error, and the insertion will fail.

Example: Inserting Data with FOREIGN KEY Constraints

Suppose you have the "Customers" and "Orders" tables as defined earlier. Here's how you can insert a new order while ensuring that it references an existing customer:

sql

-- Insert a new customer

INSERT INTO Customers (CustomerID, FirstName, LastName)

VALUES (1, 'John', 'Doe');

-- Insert a new order for the existing customer

INSERT INTO Orders (OrderID, OrderDate, CustomerID)

VALUES (101, '2023-09-14', 1);

In this sequence of SQL statements, we first insert a new customer with a `CustomerID` of 1. Then, we insert a new order for that customer, ensuring that the `CustomerID` in the "Orders" table references an existing customer.

Conclusion

The `FOREIGN KEY` constraint is a cornerstone of relational database design. It establishes relationships between tables, ensures data consistency, and maintains referential integrity. By enforcing the linkage between tables, it prevents orphaned records and inaccurate data associations. Understanding how to implement and manage foreign key constraints is crucial for building robust and reliable database systems, making it a vital concept for anyone working with SQL and databases.

6.1.3. UNIQUE Constraint

In the world of database management, maintaining data accuracy is paramount. One of the key tools for achieving this is the `UNIQUE` constraint in SQL. This constraint ensures that the values in a specified column or columns are unique across all rows in a table, preventing duplicate entries and enforcing data integrity.

Understanding the UNIQUE Constraint

The `UNIQUE` constraint is used to enforce the uniqueness of values in one or more columns in a table. It ensures that no two rows in the table have the same combination of values in the specified columns. The `UNIQUE` constraint can be applied to a single column or a combination of columns, creating a unique index on those columns to facilitate quick data retrieval.

Syntax of the UNIQUE Constraint:

sql

```
CREATE TABLE table_name
(
   column1 data_type UNIQUE,
   column2 data_type,
   ...
);
```

- `table_name`: The name of the table you're creating.

- `column1`, `column2`, ...: The columns that should have unique values.

- `data_type`: The data type of each column.

Example: Creating a Table with a UNIQUE Constraint

Suppose you want to create a "Students" table where each student's email address must be unique to avoid duplicate registrations. You can use the `UNIQUE` constraint as follows:

sql

```
CREATE TABLE Students
```

```
(
    StudentID INT PRIMARY KEY,

    FirstName VARCHAR(50),

    LastName VARCHAR(50),

    Email VARCHAR(100) UNIQUE,

    Age INT
);
```

In this example, the "Email" column is designated as having a `UNIQUE` constraint, ensuring that no two students can have the same email address.

Benefits of the UNIQUE Constraint

1. Data Integrity: The primary purpose of the `UNIQUE` constraint is to maintain data integrity by preventing duplicate values in specified columns. This ensures that the data remains accurate and consistent.

2. Efficient Data Retrieval: Columns with `UNIQUE` constraints are automatically indexed by most database management systems (DBMS). This indexing speeds up data retrieval when searching for specific values in those columns.

3. Enforcing Business Rules: UNIQUE constraints are valuable for enforcing business rules where certain data attributes must be unique. For example, email addresses, social security numbers, or product serial numbers.

4. Conflict Resolution: When an attempt is made to insert or update data that violates a `UNIQUE` constraint, the DBMS raises an error. This helps identify and resolve conflicts early in the data management process.

Inserting Data with a UNIQUE Constraint

When inserting data into a table with a `UNIQUE` constraint, you must ensure that the values in the unique column(s) are indeed unique. If you attempt to insert a record with a duplicate value in the unique column, the DBMS will raise an error, and the insertion will fail.

Example: Inserting Data with a UNIQUE Constraint

Assuming you have the "Students" table with a `UNIQUE` constraint on the "Email" column, here's how you can insert new student records while ensuring email uniqueness:

```sql
-- Insert a new student with a unique email
INSERT INTO Students (StudentID, FirstName, LastName, Email, Age)
VALUES (1, 'John', 'Doe', 'john.doe@example.com', 20);

-- Attempt to insert another student with the same email (will fail)
INSERT INTO Students (StudentID, FirstName, LastName, Email, Age)
VALUES (2, 'Jane', 'Smith', 'john.doe@example.com', 22);
```

In this sequence of SQL statements, the first insertion succeeds because the email 'john.doe@example.com' is unique. However, the second insertion attempt fails because it violates the `UNIQUE` constraint, as the same email is already in use.

Conclusion

The `UNIQUE` constraint is a fundamental tool in SQL for maintaining data accuracy and integrity. It ensures that values in specified columns remain unique, preventing duplicate entries and facilitating efficient data retrieval through indexing. By enforcing uniqueness and detecting conflicts early, the `UNIQUE` constraint is a vital concept for anyone working with databases and SQL. Understanding how to implement and manage unique constraints is key to building robust and reliable database systems.

6.1.4. CHECK Constraint

Ensuring data quality and integrity is a fundamental aspect of database design and management. The `CHECK` constraint in SQL is a powerful tool that allows you to define rules and conditions for the data stored in a column. It ensures that only valid data is inserted or updated, preventing data anomalies and errors.

Understanding the CHECK Constraint

The `CHECK` constraint is used to define rules or conditions that must be met for data in a column. These rules can be based on expressions, comparisons, or predefined functions. If data inserted or updated in a column does not satisfy the specified condition, the `CHECK` constraint prevents the operation and raises an error.

Syntax of the CHECK Constraint:

```sql
CREATE TABLE table_name
(
    column1 data_type,
    column2 data_type,
    ...
    columnN data_type CHECK (condition)
);
```

- `table_name`: The name of the table you're creating.

- `column1`, `column2`, ...: The columns where you want to apply the `CHECK` constraint.

- `data_type`: The data type of each column.

- `condition`: The condition or rule that data in the column(s) must satisfy.

Example: Creating a Table with a CHECK Constraint

Suppose you want to create a "Products" table where the price of a product must be greater than or equal to zero. You can use the `CHECK` constraint to enforce this rule:

```sql
CREATE TABLE Products
(
    ProductID INT PRIMARY KEY,
    ProductName VARCHAR(50),
```

```
    Price DECIMAL(10, 2) CHECK (Price >= 0),

    StockQuantity INT

);
```

In this example, the `CHECK` constraint is applied to the "Price" column to ensure that the price is never negative.

Benefits of the CHECK Constraint

1. Data Integrity: The primary purpose of the `CHECK` constraint is to maintain data integrity by enforcing data validation rules. This prevents the insertion or update of invalid or inconsistent data.

2. Business Rules: CHECK constraints are valuable for enforcing business-specific rules and requirements. For example, ensuring that dates are in the future, limiting the length of text fields, or enforcing numerical ranges.

3. Error Prevention: By defining validation rules at the database level, CHECK constraints prevent data anomalies and errors from corrupting the database. This adds a layer of protection to your data.

4. Consistency: CHECK constraints ensure that data remains consistent and adheres to predefined standards. This consistency is crucial for reporting, analytics, and application functionality.

Inserting Data with a CHECK Constraint

When inserting or updating data in a table with a `CHECK` constraint, you must ensure that the data satisfies the specified condition. If the condition is not met, the DBMS will raise an error, and the insertion or update will fail.

Example: Inserting Data with a CHECK Constraint

Let's consider the "Products" table with a CHECK constraint on the "Price" column, ensuring that prices are non-negative:

sql

```
-- Insert a new product with a valid price
INSERT INTO Products (ProductID, ProductName, Price, StockQuantity)
VALUES (1, 'Widget', 10.99, 100);

-- Attempt to insert a new product with a negative price (will fail)
INSERT INTO Products (ProductID, ProductName, Price, StockQuantity)
VALUES (2, 'Gadget', -5.99, 50);
```

In this example, the first insertion succeeds because the price of $10.99 is valid. However, the second insertion attempt fails because it violates the `CHECK` constraint by attempting to insert a product with a negative price.

Modifying Data with a CHECK Constraint

If you need to update data in a column with a `CHECK` constraint, you must ensure that the new data also satisfies the condition. Otherwise, the update operation will be rejected.

Example: Updating Data with a CHECK Constraint

Let's say you want to update the price of an existing product:

```sql
sql
-- Update the price of an existing product to a valid value
UPDATE Products
SET Price = 15.99
WHERE ProductID = 1;


-- Attempt to update the price of an existing product to a negative value (will fail)
UPDATE Products
SET Price = -3.99
WHERE ProductID = 1;
```

The first update succeeds because it changes the price to a valid value. However, the second update attempt fails as it violates the `CHECK` constraint.

Conclusion

The `CHECK` constraint is a valuable tool for maintaining data quality and integrity in SQL databases. It allows you to define rules and conditions that data must adhere to, preventing the insertion or update of invalid or inconsistent data. By enforcing data validation rules at the database level, CHECK constraints play a crucial role in ensuring data accuracy and reliability. Understanding how to implement and manage CHECK constraints is essential for building robust and dependable database systems.

6.2 Utilizing Indexes for Query Optimization

Efficient data retrieval is a critical aspect of database management. Indexes play a pivotal role in enhancing query performance by allowing databases to locate and retrieve data more swiftly. In this section, we will explore the significance of indexes, how they work, and how to utilize them effectively for query optimization.

Understanding Indexes

An index in a database is akin to an index in a book—it provides a means to quickly locate specific information without having to read the entire contents. In the context of databases, indexes are data structures that store a subset of the data's columns, along with a reference to the corresponding row. These data structures are organized to facilitate rapid data retrieval.

How Indexes Work

Indexes work by maintaining a sorted order of the indexed data columns, which enables the database management system (DBMS) to perform a binary search instead of scanning the entire dataset when searching for specific values. This drastically reduces the time required to locate and retrieve data.

Types of Indexes

1. Single-Column Indexes: These indexes are created on a single column of a table and are used to speed up searches on that column. They are the most common type of index.

2. Composite Indexes: Composite or multi-column indexes are created on multiple columns. They are useful when queries involve conditions on multiple columns.

3. Unique Indexes: Unique indexes ensure that the indexed columns contain unique values, preventing duplicate data in those columns.

4. Clustered Indexes: A clustered index determines the physical order of data rows in a table. Each table can have only one clustered index, as it dictates the storage structure of the entire table.

5. Non-clustered Indexes: Non-clustered indexes provide an additional way to search for data. They do not dictate the physical order of rows but contain a pointer to the actual row.

Creating Indexes

To create an index on a table, you can use SQL's `CREATE INDEX` statement. Here's a basic example:

```sql
CREATE INDEX idx_lastname ON Employees(LastName);
```

In this example, an index named `idx_lastname` is created on the "LastName" column of the "Employees" table.

Using Indexes for Query Optimization

Indexes significantly improve the speed of data retrieval operations, especially for large datasets. Here's how you can leverage indexes for query optimization:

1. Identify Query Bottlenecks: Analyze your SQL queries to identify which columns are frequently used in WHERE clauses or JOIN conditions. These are candidates for indexing.

2. Choose Columns Carefully: While indexes improve query performance, they also consume storage space and can slow down data modifications (INSERT, UPDATE, DELETE). Therefore, choose columns for indexing judiciously based on query patterns and business requirements.

3. Avoid Over-indexing: Creating indexes on every column of a table is not recommended. It can lead to excessive storage consumption and slow down data modification operations. Focus on the most frequently queried columns.

4. Use Composite Indexes: For queries involving multiple conditions, consider creating composite indexes that cover all the columns involved in the query. This reduces the need for multiple indexes and improves query performance.

5. Regularly Maintain Indexes: Indexes need maintenance over time. As data changes, indexes may become fragmented, impacting performance. Schedule regular index maintenance tasks to keep them optimized.

Example: Using an Index

Let's consider a scenario where you have a table called "Orders" with millions of rows, and you frequently need to retrieve orders by their order date. You can create an index on the "OrderDate" column to optimize such queries:

sql

```
-- Create an index on the OrderDate column
CREATE INDEX idx_orderdate ON Orders(OrderDate);
```

-- Query for orders on a specific date

SELECT * FROM Orders WHERE OrderDate = '2023-09-14';

The presence of the `idx_orderdate` index will significantly speed up the query, as the DBMS can quickly locate the relevant rows without scanning the entire table.

Conclusion

Indexes are a fundamental tool for optimizing query performance in relational databases. By efficiently organizing and accessing data, indexes reduce query response times, making database applications more responsive and efficient. However, it's essential to strike a balance between indexing and data modification performance, as excessive or improper indexing can lead to storage overhead and slower write operations. Understanding how indexes work and when to use them is crucial for database administrators and developers seeking to maximize the efficiency of their database systems.

PART VII
Advanced Queries and Data Analysis

7.1 Subqueries

Subqueries, also known as nested queries or inner queries, are a powerful feature of SQL that enable you to create complex queries by embedding one query within another. They are particularly useful when you need to retrieve data based on the results of another query. In this section, we will explore the concept of subqueries, their types, and how to use them effectively.

Understanding Subqueries

A subquery is essentially a query enclosed within parentheses and placed inside another SQL statement, such as SELECT, INSERT, UPDATE, or DELETE. The outer query is often referred to as the main query, while the inner query is the subquery. The result of the subquery is used as input for the main query.

Types of Subqueries

There are several types of subqueries, each serving a specific purpose:

1. Single-Row Subqueries: These subqueries return a single value, and they can be used in situations where you need to compare a single value to a set of values or retrieve a single result from a subquery. For example:

sql

SELECT FirstName, LastName

FROM Employees

WHERE Salary > (SELECT AVG(Salary) FROM Employees);

2. Multi-Row Subqueries: Multi-row subqueries return multiple rows of data and are used when you need to compare a set of values to another set of values or retrieve multiple results from a subquery. For example:

sql

SELECT DepartmentName

FROM Departments

WHERE DepartmentID IN (SELECT DepartmentID FROM Employees WHERE Salary > 50000);

3. Correlated Subqueries: Correlated subqueries are subqueries that refer to columns from the outer query. They are executed once for each row processed by the outer query. Correlated subqueries can be used to find related data in different tables. For example:

sql

SELECT FirstName, LastName

FROM Employees e

WHERE Salary > (SELECT AVG(Salary) FROM Employees WHERE DepartmentID = e.DepartmentID);

Using Subqueries Effectively

Subqueries can be a valuable tool for writing complex queries and performing data analysis. Here are some tips for using subqueries effectively:

1. Understand Query Execution Order: SQL databases execute subqueries before processing the main query. It's important to understand the order in which the database engine processes subqueries, especially when using correlated subqueries.

2. Use Subqueries for Filtering: Subqueries are often used to filter data based on specific conditions. You can use them in the WHERE clause of a main query to restrict the rows returned.

3. Optimize Performance: While subqueries are powerful, they can also impact query performance, especially when dealing with large datasets. Ensure that your database is properly indexed and consider optimizing your subqueries for better performance.

4. Test Subqueries: Before using subqueries in production queries, test them separately to ensure they return the expected results. This can help you catch potential issues early.

Example: Using Subqueries

Let's consider an example where you have a database of books and authors, and you want to find all authors who have written more books than the average number of books written by authors. You can use a subquery to achieve this:

```sql
SELECT AuthorName

FROM Authors

WHERE AuthorID IN (SELECT AuthorID FROM Books GROUP BY AuthorID HAVING
COUNT(BookID) > (SELECT AVG(BookCount) FROM (SELECT AuthorID,
COUNT(BookID) AS BookCount FROM Books GROUP BY AuthorID) AS Subquery));
```

In this example, the subquery calculates the average number of books written by authors and compares it with the count of books written by each author. Authors whose book count exceeds the average are returned in the result.

Conclusion

Subqueries are a fundamental part of SQL that enable you to create complex and insightful queries by embedding one query within another. They offer flexibility and power in data retrieval and analysis, allowing you to filter and manipulate data based on specific criteria. Understanding the types of subqueries and how to use them effectively is essential for anyone working with relational databases and SQL. With the ability to nest queries and perform data comparisons, subqueries are a valuable tool in your SQL toolkit for advanced data analysis and reporting.

7.2. Window Functions

Window functions are a powerful and advanced feature in SQL that allow you to perform calculations across a set of table rows related to the current row. Unlike standard aggregate functions like COUNT, SUM, AVG, etc., window functions do not reduce the number of rows in the result set. Instead, they add new columns to the result set, providing insights into data distributions, rankings, and more. In this section, we will dive into window functions, their types, and how to leverage them effectively.

Understanding Window Functions

Window functions operate over a "window" of rows defined by an OVER() clause. This window is a set of rows related to the current row, typically based on specific criteria or sorting. The result of the window function is calculated for each row in the result set, based on the data within its window.

Types of Window Functions

There are several types of window functions, each serving a different analytical purpose:

1. Ranking Functions: These functions assign a unique rank to each row within the window based on the specified order. Common ranking functions include RANK(), DENSE_RANK(), and ROW_NUMBER(). For example:

sql

```
SELECT EmployeeName, Salary, RANK() OVER (ORDER BY Salary DESC) AS SalaryRank

FROM Employees;
```

2. Aggregate Functions: Unlike traditional aggregates, window aggregate functions perform calculations across the rows in the window while keeping all rows in the result set. Examples include SUM() OVER(), AVG() OVER(), and MAX() OVER(). For example:

sql

```
SELECT ProductID, Sales, SUM(Sales) OVER (PARTITION BY Category) AS CategorySales

FROM SalesData;
```

3. Analytic Functions: Analytic functions provide insights into data distributions, such as calculating percentiles or cumulative sums. Functions like PERCENTILE_CONT() and CUME_DIST() fall into this category. For example:

sql

SELECT OrderID, Quantity, PERCENTILE_CONT(0.5) WITHIN GROUP (ORDER BY Quantity) OVER () AS MedianQuantity

FROM OrderDetails;

Using Window Functions Effectively

To make the most of window functions, consider the following best practices:

1. Understand Window Frames: Window functions allow you to define a window frame that determines which rows are included in the window. Understanding window frame specifications is crucial for accurate calculations.

2. Partition Data as Needed: The PARTITION BY clause is used to divide the result set into partitions, and window functions operate within those partitions. Use PARTITION BY to group data logically before applying window functions.

3. Order Rows Properly: Many window functions require ordering of rows within the window to be meaningful. Ensure that you use the ORDER BY clause to specify the desired row order.

4. Test and Validate: Window functions can produce complex results. Test your queries with different data scenarios to ensure they return the expected results.

Example: Using Window Functions

Suppose you have a dataset of sales transactions and want to find the total sales for each product within its category and calculate the product's sales rank within the category. You can use the SUM() and RANK() window functions as follows:

sql

```sql
SELECT ProductID, Category, Sales,
    SUM(Sales) OVER (PARTITION BY Category) AS CategorySales,
    RANK() OVER (PARTITION BY Category ORDER BY Sales DESC) AS SalesRank
FROM SalesData;
```

In this example, the SUM() function calculates the total sales for each product's category, and the RANK() function assigns a sales rank within the category based on descending sales values.

Conclusion

Window functions are a valuable tool for performing advanced analytics and gaining insights from your SQL data. They provide a way to perform calculations and aggregations while preserving the granularity of your data. Understanding the types of window functions and how to use them effectively is essential for anyone working with complex data analysis tasks. By leveraging window functions, you can gain deeper insights into your data and make more informed decisions based on your SQL queries.

7.3. Pivoting and Unpivoting Data

Pivoting and unpivoting data are essential techniques in SQL for transforming data from one shape to another. These operations are particularly useful when dealing with data that needs to be restructured for reporting, analysis, or presentation purposes. In this section, we will explore the concepts of pivoting and unpivoting, provide practical examples, and guide you through the steps to perform these operations effectively.

Pivoting Data

Pivoting data involves converting rows into columns. This is useful when you have data in a "normalized" format, where each data point is stored in a separate row, and you want to transform it into a "denormalized" format for easier analysis or reporting. Let's take a simple example:

Suppose you have a table named `Sales` with the following structure:

Product	Month	Revenue
A	January	1000
B	January	1200
A	February	1500
B	February	1600

You may want to pivot this data to have a column for each month, like this:

Product	January	February
A	1000	1500
B	1200	1600

To achieve this, you can use conditional aggregation with CASE statements:

```sql
SELECT
    Product,
    MAX(CASE WHEN Month = 'January' THEN Revenue END) AS January,
    MAX(CASE WHEN Month = 'February' THEN Revenue END) AS February
FROM Sales
GROUP BY Product;
```

In this example, we use the MAX() function along with CASE statements to pivot the data. We group the results by the `Product` column to obtain the desired pivoted format.

Unpivoting Data

Unpivoting data, on the other hand, involves converting columns into rows. This is useful when you have data in a denormalized format with multiple columns, and you want to transform it into a normalized format for further analysis or processing.

Consider the pivoted data from the previous example:

Product	January	February
A	1000	1500
B	1200	1600

You may want to unpivot this data to have a single column for the months and their respective values, like this:

Product	Month	Revenue
A	January	1000
A	February	1500
B	January	1200
B	February	1600

To achieve this, you can use the UNPIVOT operator in SQL:

```sql
SELECT Product, Month, Revenue
FROM (
    SELECT Product, January, February
    FROM PivotedSales
) AS P
UNPIVOT (
    Revenue FOR Month IN (January, February)
) AS UnpivotedSales;
```

In this example, we first select the columns we want to unpivot (January and February) and then use the UNPIVOT operator to transform the data into the desired format.

Best Practices for Pivoting and Unpivoting

1. Understand Your Data: Before pivoting or unpivoting, thoroughly understand the structure and content of your data. Ensure that the columns and values you want to work with are well-defined.

2. Choose the Right Method: Decide whether pivoting or unpivoting is the appropriate operation for your data transformation needs. Pivoting is about aggregating data, while unpivoting is about expanding it.

3. Use SQL Functions and Operators: Take advantage of SQL functions like MAX(), CASE, and the UNPIVOT operator to simplify and streamline your data transformation queries.

4. Maintain Data Integrity: Ensure that the pivoting or unpivoting process does not lead to data loss or inconsistencies. Validate the results to confirm that they align with your expectations.

5. Performance Considerations: Depending on the volume of data, these operations can be computationally expensive. Be mindful of performance implications and optimize your queries as needed.

Conclusion

Pivoting and unpivoting data are powerful techniques in SQL for restructuring data to meet specific analysis or reporting requirements. Whether you need to transform data from rows to columns or vice versa, understanding how to use SQL functions and operators for these operations is essential. By following best practices and considering your data's structure and integrity, you can effectively pivot and unpivot data to derive valuable insights and make informed decisions in your data analysis endeavors.

PART VIII
Security and Data Management

8.1 Authentication and Authorization

Authentication and authorization are critical aspects of database security, ensuring that only authorized users can access and manipulate data while maintaining data confidentiality and integrity. In this section, we will delve into the concepts of authentication and authorization in the context of SQL databases, providing practical examples and step-by-step guidance on implementing these security measures effectively.

Authentication

Authentication is the process of verifying the identity of users or applications attempting to access a database. It ensures that individuals or systems are who they claim to be before granting them access. SQL databases typically support various authentication methods, including:

1. Username and Password Authentication: This is the most common form of authentication, where users provide a valid username and password combination. To implement this method, database administrators create user accounts with associated passwords.

Example: Creating a User Account

sql

```sql
CREATE USER 'john'@'localhost' IDENTIFIED BY 'password';
```

2. Integrated Windows Authentication: Some databases, such as Microsoft SQL Server, offer integrated Windows authentication, where users are authenticated based on their Windows user accounts. This method is often preferred in Windows-based environments.

3. Multi-Factor Authentication (MFA): MFA adds an extra layer of security by requiring users to provide multiple forms of identification, such as a password and a one-time code sent to their mobile device.

Authorization

Authorization determines what actions users or applications are allowed to perform within the database once they have been authenticated. It defines access rights and permissions, ensuring that users can only interact with data and perform operations they are authorized to do. Common authorization mechanisms include:

1. Role-Based Access Control (RBAC): RBAC assigns permissions to roles, and users are associated with specific roles. This simplifies permission management and allows for granular access control.

Example: Creating a Role and Granting Permissions

sql

CREATE ROLE 'sales_team';

GRANT SELECT ON 'sales_data' TO 'sales_team';

2. Access Control Lists (ACLs): ACLs define access permissions at the individual level, specifying which users or roles can access specific objects or perform specific operations.

3. Row-Level Security: Some databases support row-level security, where users are only allowed to access specific rows of data within a table based on defined criteria.

Implementing Authentication and Authorization

Let's walk through the process of implementing authentication and authorization in an SQL database using MySQL as an example.

Step 1: Create User Accounts

To create user accounts with username and password authentication, you can use SQL commands like `CREATE USER` and `GRANT`.

Example: Creating a User Account

sql

CREATE USER 'john'@'localhost' IDENTIFIED BY 'password';

Step 2: Define Roles and Permissions

Next, define roles and associated permissions using `CREATE ROLE` and `GRANT`.

Example: Creating a Role and Granting Permissions

sql

CREATE ROLE 'sales_team';

GRANT SELECT ON 'sales_data' TO 'sales_team';

Step 3: Associate Users with Roles

Associate users with specific roles to grant them the corresponding permissions.

Example: Associating a User with a Role

sql

GRANT 'sales_team' TO 'john'@'localhost';

Step 4: Implement Additional Security Measures

Consider implementing additional security measures such as MFA, encrypted connections (SSL/TLS), and auditing to enhance database security further.

Example: Enforcing MFA

sql

ALTER USER 'john'@'localhost' REQUIRE MULTI-FACTOR AUTHENTICATION;

Conclusion

Authentication and authorization are fundamental components of database security, safeguarding your data against unauthorized access and ensuring that users only have the necessary permissions. By following best practices and leveraging the built-in security features of your database system, you can create a robust security framework to protect your valuable data assets. Always stay up to date with security patches and conduct regular security audits to mitigate potential vulnerabilities and ensure the ongoing integrity of your database system.

8.2. Backup and Recovery

Data is a critical asset for any organization, and ensuring its availability and integrity is paramount. To protect your data from loss or corruption, you must have a robust backup and recovery strategy in place. This section will guide you through the process of implementing effective backup and recovery procedures for your SQL database.

Backup Strategies

Before delving into the technical aspects of backup and recovery, it's essential to understand the different types of backups and when to use them:

1. Full Backup: A full backup contains a copy of the entire database and is performed periodically, such as daily or weekly. It provides a complete snapshot of the database at a specific point in time.

2. Differential Backup: A differential backup captures changes made since the last full backup. It is faster and requires less storage space than a full backup but may take longer than other types of backups.

3. Incremental Backup: Incremental backups capture changes made since the last backup, whether it's a full, differential, or incremental backup. These backups are the smallest in size but may require more effort during recovery.

4. Transaction Log Backup: Transaction log backups capture changes to the database's transaction log. They are crucial for point-in-time recovery and are typically done frequently, often every few minutes.

Creating Backups

Now, let's walk through creating backups using SQL commands, focusing on a Microsoft SQL Server example.

Step 1: Full Backup

sql

```
BACKUP DATABASE YourDatabaseName TO DISK =
'C:\Backup\YourDatabaseFullBackup.bak';
```

Step 2: Differential Backup

sql

```
BACKUP DATABASE YourDatabaseName TO DISK =
'C:\Backup\YourDatabaseDifferentialBackup.bak' WITH DIFFERENTIAL;
```

Step 3: Incremental Backup

sql

```
BACKUP DATABASE YourDatabaseName TO DISK =
'C:\Backup\YourDatabaseIncrementalBackup.bak' WITH DIFFERENTIAL;
```

Step 4: Transaction Log Backup

sql

BACKUP LOG YourDatabaseName TO DISK = 'C:\Backup\YourDatabaseLogBackup.trn';

These SQL commands create backups of your database and transaction logs, which you should store securely, preferably offsite or in a remote location.

Recovery Strategies

Having backups is essential, but knowing how to recover from them is equally critical. Here's how to perform recovery, again using Microsoft SQL Server as an example:

Step 1: Restore Full Backup

sql

RESTORE DATABASE YourDatabaseName FROM DISK = 'C:\Backup\YourDatabaseFullBackup.bak' WITH REPLACE;

Step 2: Restore Differential Backup

sql

RESTORE DATABASE YourDatabaseName FROM DISK = 'C:\Backup\YourDatabaseDifferentialBackup.bak' WITH NORECOVERY;

Step 3: Restore Incremental Backup (if applicable)

sql

```sql
RESTORE DATABASE YourDatabaseName FROM DISK =
'C:\Backup\YourDatabaseIncrementalBackup.bak' WITH NORECOVERY;
```

Step 4: Restore Transaction Log Backups

sql

```sql
RESTORE LOG YourDatabaseName FROM DISK =
'C:\Backup\YourDatabaseLogBackup1.trn' WITH NORECOVERY;
```

```sql
RESTORE LOG YourDatabaseName FROM DISK =
'C:\Backup\YourDatabaseLogBackup2.trn' WITH RECOVERY;
```

These SQL commands restore your database to a specific point in time, using the full, differential, and transaction log backups you created. Be sure to follow the correct order and use the `WITH NORECOVERY` or `WITH RECOVERY` options accordingly.

Automating Backups

Manually creating backups can be error-prone and time-consuming. Most database management systems offer tools and features to automate backups. For example, in Microsoft SQL Server, you can set up Maintenance Plans or use SQL Server Agent to schedule regular backups.

Monitoring and Testing

Regularly monitor your backup processes to ensure they are running correctly. Additionally, perform test restores from backups to validate their integrity and practice recovery scenarios. Testing is crucial to ensuring that you can recover your data when needed.

Offsite and Cloud Backups

Consider storing backups offsite or in the cloud for added redundancy and disaster recovery preparedness. Cloud storage providers like Amazon S3, Azure Blob Storage, or Google Cloud Storage offer reliable and scalable options for storing backup files securely.

Conclusion

Implementing a robust backup and recovery strategy is essential for safeguarding your SQL database. By understanding backup types, creating regular backups, and practicing recovery procedures, you can minimize data loss and downtime in case of unexpected events. Regularly review and update your backup strategy to adapt to changing requirements and technology advancements, ensuring the continuity of your data-driven operations.

8.3. Handling Incidents and Logging

Incident handling and logging are critical components of database security and data management. In this section, we will explore how to effectively handle security incidents and the importance of comprehensive logging in your SQL database.

Incident Handling

Incidents, such as security breaches or data breaches, can occur despite your best efforts to secure your SQL database. Being prepared to respond swiftly and effectively is crucial to minimize damage and prevent future incidents. Here's a step-by-step guide on how to handle a security incident:

Step 1: Detection

Detecting an incident is the first step. This can be done through various means, including intrusion detection systems, monitoring tools, or reports from users or administrators.

Step 2: Containment

Once an incident is detected, the next priority is to contain it. Isolate affected systems, disable compromised accounts, or take other actions to prevent further damage.

Step 3: Eradication

After containment, identify the root cause of the incident and eliminate it. Patch vulnerabilities, remove malware, or fix misconfigurations that allowed the incident to occur.

Step 4: Recovery

With the threat eliminated, you can begin the process of restoring affected systems and data from backups. Ensure that the recovery process is well-documented and tested.

Step 5: Investigation

Conduct a thorough investigation to understand the scope of the incident, how it occurred, and what data or systems were affected. This step is critical for preventing future incidents.

Step 6: Communication

Communicate the incident to relevant stakeholders, including affected individuals, legal authorities, and regulatory bodies, if required. Transparency is essential to maintain trust.

Step 7: Documentation

Document all actions taken during the incident response process. This documentation will be valuable for post-incident analysis and reporting.

Logging Best Practices

Comprehensive logging is essential for both incident detection and post-incident analysis. Here are some best practices for logging in your SQL database:

1. Enable Auditing: Most modern database systems offer auditing features that allow you to track and log specific database activities, including logins, queries, and modifications.

2. Log Retention: Define a log retention policy that specifies how long log data should be retained. Consider legal and regulatory requirements when setting this policy.

3. Log Integrity: Ensure that log files are protected from tampering or unauthorized access. Implement access controls and encryption for log files.

4. Log Analysis: Regularly review and analyze log data to detect suspicious or anomalous activities. Consider using log analysis tools and security information and event management (SIEM) systems.

5. Alerting: Implement real-time alerting for critical events. Set up alerts for specific log entries that may indicate a security breach or other important database events.

6. User Activity Tracking: Track user activity, including failed login attempts, to identify potential security threats. Monitor for unusual login patterns.

7. Error Logging: Capture and log error messages and exceptions to identify issues with database performance or security.

8. Centralized Logging: Consider centralizing logs from multiple database instances to streamline monitoring and analysis.

Log Querying Example

Let's look at a SQL example of querying database logs for suspicious activity:

```sql
-- Find failed login attempts
SELECT username, event_type, event_time
FROM security_logs
WHERE event_type = 'login_failure'
ORDER BY event_time DESC;

-- Identify users with unusual login patterns
SELECT username, COUNT(*) AS login_attempts
FROM security_logs
GROUP BY username
HAVING login_attempts > 10;
```

These queries can help you identify potential security threats or unusual user behavior by analyzing the database logs.

Conclusion

Handling security incidents and maintaining comprehensive logs are essential aspects of managing a secure SQL database environment. By following incident handling procedures and implementing robust logging practices, you can detect, respond to, and recover from security incidents effectively. Regularly review and update your incident response plan and logging practices to adapt to changing threats and compliance requirements, ensuring the security and integrity of your database.

Conclusion
Becoming a SQL Expert!

As we conclude our journey through the world of SQL with the book **"Learning SQL: Master SQL Fundamentals,"** we want to express our sincere gratitude to you, our valued reader. We hope that this book has been an insightful and practical guide in your quest to master SQL fundamentals and become a proficient SQL user.

Becoming a SQL expert is not just about learning a programming language; it's about gaining a powerful tool for managing and querying data effectively. SQL is the foundation of modern data-driven applications, and your newfound skills are bound to open doors to exciting career opportunities in fields ranging from data analysis and business intelligence to software development and database administration.

We encourage you to continue your SQL journey beyond this book. Explore advanced SQL topics, dive into specific database management systems, and tackle real-world projects. The SQL community is vast and supportive, with numerous resources and communities ready to assist you in your learning and problem-solving endeavors.

Remember that mastering SQL is an ongoing process. Stay curious, keep practicing, and never stop learning. Whether you're working with databases for personal projects, academic research, or in a professional capacity, the knowledge and skills you've gained will be invaluable.

Thank you for choosing **"Learning SQL: Master SQL Fundamentals"** as your companion on this journey. We wish you every success as you apply your SQL expertise and embark on new adventures in the world of data.

Happy querying, and may your databases always return the results you seek!